Law and Economics
for Landlines Telecommunications

European University Studies

Europäische Hochschulschriften

Publications Universitaires Européennes

Series V

Economics and Management

Reihe V Série V

Volks- und Betriebswirtschaft

Sciences économiques, gestion d'entreprise

Vol./Bd. 2812

PETER LANG

Frankfurt am Main · Berlin · Bern · Bruxelles · New York · Oxford · Wien

Albrecht von Breitenbuch

Law and Economics for Landlines Telecommunications

Liberalisation, Regulation and Deregulation in Germany

PETER LANG
Europäischer Verlag der Wissenschaften

Die Deutsche Bibliothek - CIP-Einheitsaufnahme

Breitenbuch, Albrecht / von:

Law and economics for landlines telecommunications : liberalisation, regulation and deregulation in Germany / Albrecht von Breitenbuch. - Frankfurt am Main ; Berlin ; Bern ; Bruxelles ; New York ; Oxford ; Wien : Lang, 2001
(European university studies : Ser. 5, Economics and management ; Vol. 2812)
ISBN 3-631-38613-3

ISSN 0531-7339
ISBN 3-631-38613-3
US-ISBN 0-8204-5444-3

www.peterlang.de

PREFACE

Over three years ago Germany took the last and most important step towards liberalisation in the market for public landlines telecommunications. When monopoly for voice telephony was eventually lifted on 1 January 1998 this was only the final point of a long process to liberalise this market.

This particular market is of great interest from a legal as well as from an economic point of view. On the grounds of economic thought the provision of telecommunication services had traditionally been regarded as a natural monopoly, which should be under sole control of the state to guarantee best coverage and highest efficiency at lowest prices. Hence over time the German state had established a legal environment in order to protect this monopoly and to exclude market entry.

However, as other countries like the United Kingdom or the U. S. had made some very promising steps towards a more open market this traditional concept for the telecommunication market began to crumble. Due to advances in technology and far greater demand for telecommunication services the maintenance of monopoly had lost its main justification as the market concept seemed to work successfully and provided benefits from competition to society.

To establish lasting competition different countries followed different strategies. For example, in the U. S. the monopolistic incumbent was split into several independent companies. Germany's strategy was to privatise the monopolist Deutsche Telekom and to encourage new entry from private companies. To this end a complex, new legal environment had to be formed to allow for entry and fair competition as well as for regulation if necessary. But once economic forces and technology had been given their full scope for market power they added their own special momentum to the process.

The aim of this book is to give an overview over the market for public landlines telecommunications in Germany with a focus on past legal and economic developments towards competition. Most recently this market has changed from state monopoly to a regulated, but highly competitive and diversified marketplace. This book evaluates the process with regards to both its legal and economic aspects. After considerable progress in liberalisation and regulation of the market it is now time to enter the stage of deregulation for a prosperous future for German telecommunications.

The text is based on a dissertation submitted to the University of Durham, England, for the degree of Master of Arts in Managerial Economics in September 2000. Some alterations were necessary in wording and format for this publication. As the findings of the dissertation have stood the proof of time so far there was no need for updating all tables and figures with the latest numbers.

My special thanks go to Mr. Kevin Lawler as my lecturer and supervisor in the Department of Economics & Finance in Durham. He encouraged me in my choice of topic from the beginning and gave me patient and very helpful guidance as the work proceeded.

Berlin, May 2001 *Albrecht von Breitenbuch*

TABLE OF CONTENTS

3 The Market for Landlines Telecommunications

1 Introduction

1.1 The Importance of Telecommunications

At the turn of the millennium telecommunications play a key role for economic prosperity and development for all nations. The importance of telecommunications derives from its supportive role for almost any economic activity. Increasing division of labour on a national and global scale requires an increasing coordination in production and supply of goods and services.

Telecommunication networks form the backbones of the modern 'information society', as they spread technology, knowledge and innovation to any place on Earth. Only ten years ago the telecommunication sector in Europe was still characterised by national exclusive rights. After fundamental reforms and legislation a new market emerged with fierce competition. The once separated and now converging sectors of telecommunications, media and information technology are expected to change almost all aspects of private and professional life over time. The market includes many of the world's largest companies and is growing at a high rate. Not only has this made telecommunications one of the stock market's favourites and leading indicators. Moreover its unique importance has placed it in the focus of society and politics. Successful progress in telecommunications is vital for the competitiveness of nations. As Germany is the biggest single economy within Europe her progress and success has had and will have a strong impact on the whole European Union and other nations.

1.2 Definitions of Terms

The terms *liberalisation*, *regulation* and *deregulation* are used differently in literature and need to be defined. *Liberalisation* shall mean the process of opening a state monopoly to competition by liberalising first of all legislation. Once market entry is allowed, *regulation* will rule and interfere in market decisions until fair and sufficient competition is established. At this stage regulation shall be phasing out towards *deregulation.*

Technical terms shall be used according to Sec. 3 of the German Telecommunications Act (TKG)[1]. *Telecommunications* shall mean

> "the technical process of sending, transmitting and receiving any kind of message in the form of signs, voice, images or sounds by means of any...capable technical equipment" (Sec. 3 No. 15, 16 TKG).

This definition distinguishes between three levels of telecommunications: networks, services and terminal equipment[2]. *Telecommunication landlines* shall be defined as

> "underground or overhead telecommunications cable systems, including the associated switching and distribution equipment, poles and supports, cable chambers and cable duct conduits" (Sec. 3 No. 19 TKG).

On a final note it has to be stressed that the translation of technical terms from German into English is not uniform in literature. In the following text English phrases with the common German abbreviations are used, but if any doubt the reader is advised to look at the table of abbreviations and technical terms towards the back of this book, where the exact German terms are given. For background information appendices are included after the main text.

1.3 Aim and Objective

The aim of this book is to evaluate the process of changes in a particular market on the transition from monopoly to competition. The German market of public landlines telecommunications provided a good example for such an analysis as it had been opened for new entrants only about three years ago. Therefore, most recently it had passed through the stages of liberalisation and regulation towards deregulation.

---

[1] English version of Act obtainable under http://www.regtp.de/en/gesetze/start/fs_04.html

[2] Like *Krüger/ Tetens/ Voß* (1995) pp. 15 – 18 and *Mahrdt* (1998) p. 23, sometimes 'certification' is regarded as a fourth sub-sector of telecommunications [*Pfeiffer/ Wieland* (1990) p. 32].

Such a process requires most fundamental adjustments in the legal framework as well as in economic policy and challenges all present and potential players in the market to find their new positions. In this course of action the impact of the actual forces driving this market from the outside or the inside became visible. With *Bain*'s simplistic *Structure-Conduct-Performance approach*[3] in mind, this piece of work shall reveal how the grid of links between market structure and competitors' conduct and performance depend on and simultaneously form their legal and competitive environment. On the ground of this analysis the process of liberalisation as a whole shall be evaluated and perspectives for the future can be given.

As this work is based on a dissertation which was restricted in time and words this text focuses on the general developments and interrelations within the market and its global landscape. It covers a time span from the early 1990s up to September 2000 with focus on development since January 1998 when monopoly was finally lifted for landlines voice telephony.

1.4 Structure of the Text

To achieve this aim and objective this text follows in its structure the same way as research for the dissertation proceeded:

This introductory chapter points at the importance of telecommunications in modern society and economics. It further presents definitions for the analysis. Passages on aim and objective and structure shall help the reader to follow the research methods employed.

The following two chapters reflect the two forces, which have mainly driven and are still driving German telecommunications: its legal and its economic environment. The second chapter analyses the legal evolution through three major legislative acts for liberalisation and regulation. This shall provide the reader with an understanding of the legal framework within which market developments occurred. The third chapter examines the market covering barriers to entry, technology supply, customer demand, substitutes, and competitive structure. Since both the German legislation and the market are strongly affected

[3] See *Stead/ Curwen/ Lawler* (1996) pp. 4 – 8 for details on this approach.

by international developments each chapter includes a section on European and global aspects.

The fourth chapter concentrates on the incumbent Deutsche Telekom. It shows the company's progress from monopolist to competitor, from public administration to private entrepreneurship as it has been exposed to changes in both legal and economic environment.

The fifth chapter on regulation and deregulation outlines the links surrounding the Regulatory Authority and its regulatory measures as well as chances for deregulation.

The concluding chapter presents the findings of this analysis. It gives an evaluation of the liberalisation process based on these findings and shows some perspectives for future developments. This section also points at limitations of this work and possible next steps for future research.

1.5 Research Methods

Research for this work followed a literature-based approach. Sources from public libraries, databases, companies and Internet were used to collect information and data on legislation, markets and companies. Official reports are often available in English and were of great help. A considerable amount of research activity was spent in libraries in Berlin, Germany, especially on German legal literature. However, since telecommunications is exposed to a rapidly changing environment of technology, law and market forces, often only recent literature was useful. Public libraries seem to have difficulties keeping their stocks of such fast developing fields for research up-dated. But the literature found seems by any means to be sufficient to draw the main lines of recent and near future development in German telecommunications.

Even though the legal and economic environment is analysed in general terms some parts concentrate on Deutsche Telekom and its main national and international competitors. Despite the recognised fact that telecommunications offer important opportunities for small and medium sized firms this focus on large firms seemed justified for two reasons: first, only performance of Deutsche Telekom can be tracked back beyond 1998 due to its existence in monopoly.

Secondly, during the research it became very obvious that the large firms, and Deutsche Telekom as the major player in particular, are driving the market and influence public policy and law.

In the tables, U.K. figures are often shown for better compatibility for readers with a non-German background. For clarity, figures are always given in the currency used by the particular source.

2 The Law for Telecommunications

2.1 Development towards Monopoly[4]

In Germany, state monopoly in telecommunications dates back a long history as in most German territories an entirely stately owned and run postal service had existed for centuries. Territorial governments used new messaging technologies like electrical telegraphy for their military and administrative purposes. Since telegraphy was not profitable, territorial authorities were the only providers. Consequently, in most territories state monopolies of telegraphy were established by mere facts without any legislative act, easily protected by exclusive public rights-of-ways.

After the creation of the unified German Empire in 1871, a single network was established and posts and telegraphy were merged within the *Reichspost* in 1875 in order to cross-subsidise telegraphy with high postal profits. The Telegraphy Act of 1891/92 (TelG) became the first legislative basis for state monopoly, which could be applied and expanded to new technologies like telephony by broad definitions[5].

Under the Weimar Constitution of 1919, Art. 6 No. 7 and Art. 88, the Empire was entitled to legislative and administrative power in telegraphy and telephony. Inventions and technical improvements made it necessary to replace the TelG by the Telecommunications Installations Act (FAG) in 1927/28.

---

[4] As main reference for this section see: *Sprißler* (1991) pp. 159 – 177.

[5] *RGSt* Vol. 19, p. 55 (57): telegraphy is any method to transmit messages over a distance, no matter whether electrical or pneumatic force or optical or acoustic signals are used.

2.2 Telecommunications under ruling of Deutsche Bundespost

After the Second World War the West German Constitution (GG) adopted the articles from the Weimar Constitution regarding telegraphy and telephony to continue state monopoly (Art. 73 No. 7 and Art. 87 Para. 1 GG). For telecommunications the FAG remained in force until 1996 with *Deutsche Bundespost* (DBP) succeeding the *Reichspost*[6]. The very broad definition of '*Fernmeldeanlage*'[7] in Sec. 1 FAG made it possible to extend this monopoly for new inventions and improvements under DBP's very protective policy[8]. By 1989 DBP enjoyed monopoly across all market levels of networks, services and terminal equipment including certification, heavily guarded by the Constitution.

DBP was structured as a largely autonomous administration headed by the Federal Ministry of Posts and Telecommunications (BMPT). For fiscal reasons, DBP was distinguished from other federal administrations by its economic independence as a so-called special fund, which excluded tax liability and participation in the federal budget, but DBP had to make considerable contributions[9]. The BMPT served a double role: regulatory body for the whole telecommunication industry as well as management for DBP. Compromises were, therefore, often made in political and economic decisions or administrative and commercial functions. This is very much reflected in consistence and power of the Administrative Council as shown in Figure 2.1 whose decisions were binding for the minister.

As a federal administrative body DBP's actions had to be based on laws and law-like rules. Moreover, the majority of its employees had the status of civil servants granting special employment and pension rights. As a whole, institutional and regulatory constraints were complex and numerous.

---

[6] Mass communication through radio and television was handed over to the rule of the Federal States.

[7] Translation: telecommunications installation

[8] *Pfeiffer/ Wieland* (1990) pp. 22 – 25.

[9] *Pfeiffer/ Wieland* (1990) p. 7.

Figure 2.1: The Administrative Council of Deutsche Bundespost[10]

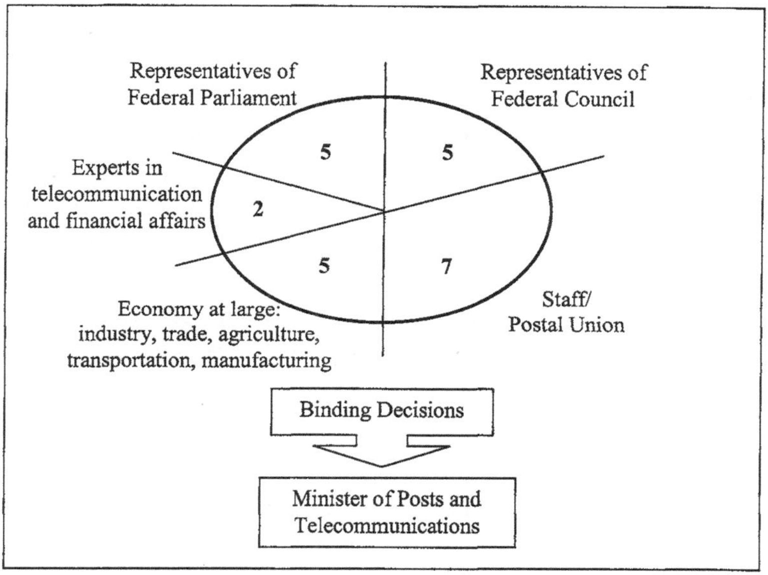

2.3 The Postal Reform I, 1989: Restructuring

The first step towards liberalisation of the German telecommunication market was the 1989 reform, the so-called 'Postal Reform I'[11].

2.3.1 Motives and Objectives

The main objective of this reform was to introduce more flexibility by means of competition into posts and telecommunications. A new structure intended to shape DBP towards a more market orientated, efficient and flexible organisation. However, under political pressure especially from the then powerful Postal Union many desirable changes could not be set into force[12].

[10] *Pfeiffer/ Wieland* (1990) p. 8.
[11] See also 'Chronology of Liberalisation' in Appendix 1.
[12] *Pfeiffer/ Wieland* (1990) pp. 12.

2.3.2 Separation of regulatory from entrepreneurial Functions

The first Postal Reform resulted in the separation of the regulatory from the entrepreneurial functions of DBP. The special fund of DBP was split up into DBP Postdienst (postal services), DBP Telekom (telecommunication services) and DBP Postbank (banking services). Run as profit centres each of these entities was granted a small degree of entrepreneurial independence with its own boards[13]. As a consequence services of the other entities had to be paid for at full costs, but cross subsidisation on DBP directorate level was still possible. DBP's contribution to the federal budget became equal to the tax burden it would have to pay. Important for customers was that from then onwards civil law would be applicable to their legal relations with DBP. Nevertheless all three remained public enterprises employing civil servants[14].

2.3.3 Competition on certain Submarkets

The market of terminal equipment was completely deregulated. Only for safety reasons all equipment needed to be type-approved by an independent laboratory under authority of the BMPT[15] or any other EC-country. All services were opened to competition including cable TV, satellite systems and mobile communications, with the significant exception of both the voice telephony service and the establishment and provision of landlines networks[16]. Voice telephone services, however, made up for over 90% of German telecommunication business[17].

---

[13] *Scherer/ Ellinghaus* (1998) pp. 134 – 135. For new structure see Appendix 2.

[14] *Börnsen* (1996) p. 324.

[15] Mainly the ZZF, in 1992 renamed as BZT, which merged with the BAPT in 1996, see Appendix 4.

[16] To compensate infrastructural obligations whose political importance is highlighted by the replacement of the Administrative Council with the Infrastructure Council increasing power of the Federal States.

[17] *Pfeiffer/ Wieland* (1990) p. 18.

2.4 The Postal Reform II, 1994: Privatising

In 1994 the German Federal Parliament adopted legislation, which was aimed at the privatisation of DBP's three enterprises.

2.4.1 Motives and Objectives

Since the first reform did not allow full flexibility a further reform became necessary[18]. International telecommunications were changing rapidly[19] and in 1993 an EU Council Resolution proclaimed entire liberalisation of the telecommunication market[20]. In preparation for open markets and globalisation DBP enterprises needed independence from politics and a focus on entrepreneurship. A strong position in the financial markets was vital especially for DBP Telekom to cover investments after German reunification in 1990 as well as future international acquisitions. To this end, these enterprises were transformed into stock corporations.

2.4.2 Constitutional Changes

The organisational privatisation of DBP Telekom, which took effect on 1 January 1995, was initially not accompanied by any further liberalisation. Instead, the successor *Deutsche Telekom AG* (DT) was allowed to maintain its monopoly over fixed lines networks until August 1996 and its exclusive right to provide voice telephony services until January 1998[21]. Nevertheless, from the legal point of view the Postal Reform II with fundamental changes of the GG[22] and new and amending legislation[23] was the core of the liberalisation process.

---

[18] *Börnsen* (1996) pp. 324 – 325.

[19] The U.S., Japan and the U.K. had allowed privatisation and competition since the early 1980s, *Schwintowski* (1998) pp. 16.

[20] For this see Section 2.6.1 on European Law.

[21] *Scherer/ Ellinghaus* (1998) p. 135.

[22] For full text of the relevant articles, especially Art. 87f and 143b GG, see Appendix 3.

[23] Overview of PT Restructuring Act (PTNeuOG) given by *Königshofen* (1995) pp. 112 – 116.

In order to privatise both task and organisation of telecommunications two fundamental changes were necessary: first, Art. 87 Para. 1 GG had to be altered as it guaranteed services for telecommunications as a federal task[24]. The amendment of Art. 87f GG marks

> "die Verlagerung...von der Versorgung mit Leistungen zur Sicherstellung der Erbringung von Leistungen"[25].

The Constitution protects consumers by a guarantee for comprehensive and adequate coverage with telecommunication services. Future services shall be organised as private law activities by businesses succeeding DBP and other private providers. This excludes the Federation from any future business activity in this area and guarantees equality in competition to all providers[26].

Secondly, the organisational transformation of DBP Telekom into a private law company is outlined in Art. 143b GG. All exclusive rights over telecommunications were relegated to DT for the time being. Most fundamental and controversial, however, was the future of DBP's 306,000 federal civil servants, as civil servants had never been allowed in private businesses fulfilling private tasks[27]. The so-called '*Beleihungsmodell*'[28] was introduced: DT employed DBP Telekom's civil servants, preserving their legal position and responsibility of their former employer. At the same time DT was conferred with the same rights as the former employer. This model gave DT higher flexibility in salary and contracts and the opportunity to retain their workforce without costly buy-outs, but on the burden of high pension payments.

Unchanged, but obviously affected was the basic right for secrecy of telecommunications as guaranteed under Art. 10 GG. Basic rights allow citizens to defend themselves only against state authority. However, the state is also obliged to protect its citizens from private third parties. Therefore, even if a private company cannot be required directly to protect people's basic rights people can still claim government to force them to do so by appropriate law. In

---

[24] *Schmidt* (1993) pp. 965 – 976.

[25] *Benz* (1998) p. 140. Translation: the shift ... from state supply of services towards state guarantee of such services.

[26] *Rottmann* (1994) pp. 194 – 195.

[27] *Ossenbühl/ Ritgen* (1999) pp. 24 – 29.

[28] Translation: Conferment Model. Later also used in privatisation of DBP Postdienst, DBP Postbank and Deutsche Bundesbahn (Federal Railways).

this respect the basic right changed its nature from a guarantee of direct to indirect protection[29].

2.4.3 New Structure and Control under the Stock Company Act[30]

The BMPT remained the central regulatory body supported by the Federal Department for Posts and Telecommunications (BAPT) and the Federal Department for Certification in Telecommunications (BZT), which were merged in 1996[31]. The Regulatory Council replaced the former Infrastructure Council with representatives of Federal Parliament and Federal Council.

For economic control over the three new private law companies the Federal Institution for Posts and Telecommunications DBP (BAnstPT) was founded[32]. Its tasks are to exercise the Federation's shareholder rights under the Stock Company Act, to support the companies on their way to going public[33], and to co-ordinate the business of the three enterprises.

2.5 The Telecommunications Act, 1996: Opening the Market

The 1996 Telecommunications Act (TKG[34]), sometimes misleadingly titled as 'Postal Reform III'[35], provides the legal framework for the newly liberalised market.

---

[29] *Rottmann* (1994) p. 196.
[30] See Appendix 4.
[31] *Benz* (1998) p. 141.
[32] *Herres* (1994) pp. 302 – 308.
[33] DT has been listed since November 1996, Deutsche Post AG had their IPO in November 2000.
[34] An English version of the TKG is obtainable under: http://www.regtp.de/en/gesetze/start/fs_04.html
[35] *Bötsch* (1996) p. 4.

2.5.1 Motives and Objectives

European liberalisation policy[36] and earlier reform steps not reaching far enough made further legislation inevitable. During the Postal Reform II the FAG had been set out of force by 1998 anyway[37]. The TKG is aimed to balance interests of users, of public safety and of competitors in a free market beginning in January 1998[38].

2.5.2 Contents of the Act[39]

The Act is based on the – unwritten – principle that everybody has the right to offer telecommunication services, which is enshrined in the constitutional 'Right to choose an occupation'[40].

- **Market entry:**[41]

  Any provider of telecommunication services has to notify the Regulatory Authority of the operation. A licence is only required for the operation of transmission lines beyond the border of a single property if used for public telecommunication services (licence classes 1 to 3[42]) and for offering voice telephony on the basis of self-operated networks (licence class 4). Any

  > "applicant... [has to prove its] reliability, efficiency and specialised knowledge required ... exercis[ing] the licence rights applied for in order to ensure ... lasting"

  performance[43]. This scheme allows for case-by-case regulation as well as safeguarding of universal services.

---

[36] For more detail see Section 2.6.1 on European Law.
[37] *Scheuerle/ Lehr/ Mayen* (1997) p. 2.
[38] Sec. 2 Para. 2 TKG, *Schrader* (1996) pp. 35 – 36.
[39] As main reference for this section see: *Scherer/ Ellinghaus* (1998).
[40] Art. 12 Para. 1 GG, *Scherer/ Ellinghaus* (1998) p. 136.
[41] See Sec. 6 – 16 TKG.
[42] Licence class 1: public mobile radio service; class 2: public satellite services; class 3: other telecommunication service requiring a licence.
[43] Sec. 8 Para. 3 TKG; *Scheuerle/ Lehr/ Mayen* (1997) p. 5.

- **Universal Services:**[44]

  Under the TKG, universal services are defined as

  > "a minimum offering of public telecommunication services...[of] a particular quality...at an affordable price".

  As ensured in the Constitution, the TKG establishes a regulatory framework for the provision of universal services. It is expected that such services will be provided within competition[45], but if necessary, they will be funded by a charge imposed on all companies operating in the relevant market so that not a single provider has to bear the burden.

- **Regulation:**[46]

  The TKG contains sector-specific rules on price regulation in order to prevent abusive behaviour by a dominant operator, including cross-subsidisation and other form of discriminatory pricing. If a licensee under class 3 or 4 has a dominant position, its prices and price-related components of general terms and conditions require prior approval by the Regulatory Authority.

- **Open Network Provision (ONP) and Interconnection:**[47]

  To ensure the nation-wide provision of services and fair and effective competition dominant providers are required to grant their competitors non-discriminatory access to their services (ONP) as well as to their network or parts thereof (interconnection).

- **Scarce Resources:**[48]

  The TKG also refers to the allocation of scarce resources, which are vita for effective competition. Rules on numbering ensure number portabilit and carrier preselection. For effective, interference-free use of frequencies,

---

[44] See Sec. 17 – 22 TKG.
[45] *Federal Parliament* (1996).
[46] See Sec. 23 – 33 TKG.
[47] See Sec. 34 – 39 TKG.
[48] See Sec. 43 – 58 TKG.

a regulatory framework of administration and allocation is established. The licensee is granted free use of public ways for installation of telecommunication lines. Even private property may be crossed if it only has an immaterial impact, but compensation may be required[49].

- **Consumer Protection[50] and Data Protection[51]:**

  As one of the legislative primary objectives, consumer protection rules within the TKG and complementing ordinances content the liability of providers for claims, information requirements, procedures and time limits for changes in offer, and requirements for billing and rate level verification. Rules on personal data protection ensure the constitutional right of telecommunication secrecy.

2.5.3 The Regulatory Authority for Telecommunications and Posts

When the BMPT ceased to exist after 31 December 1997 ownership rights together with the BAnstPT were transferred to the Federal Ministry of Finance. Both BMPT and BAPT[52] assumed their duties to the new Regulatory Authority (RegTP). This sector-specific regulatory body operates under suspicy of the Federal Ministry for Economics and Technology, independently of the Federal Cartel Office[53].

The RegTP[54]

> "is tasked with promoting the development of the postal and telecommunications markets through liberalisation and deregulation. ...The former monopoly

[49] The Federal High Court awarded compensation to a private landowner when telecommunication lines were built or even replaced along existing electric power lines, *FAZ* (15/07/2000) p. 14.
[50] See Sec. 40 – 42 TKG.
[51] See Sec. 85 – 93 TKG.
[52] Certification and approval of transmitting equipment now under Sec. 59 – 65 TKG.
[53] For today's structure of regulation see Appendix 5.
[54] See Sec. 66 – 84 TKG, as reference and for more information see RegTP homepage in English under http://www.regtp.de/en/behoerde/start/fs_01.html

> operators..., Deutsche Post AG and DT, will be able to maintain their dominant position long after market liberalisation."

State regulation is therefore regarded necessary to

> "check on each dominant provider's position in the market and to create a level playing field"

for fair competition. This

> "regulatory approach...goes beyond merely policing anti-competitive behaviour ex post...[and is] too specialised to be fulfilled under general competition law"[55].

As long as failure in these markets occurs there will be a need for sector-specific regulation.

The RegTP is headed by a president and two vice-presidents who are appointed by the Federal Government upon proposal of an Advisory Council. This consists of nine representatives of each legislative chamber replacing the former Regulatory Council and participates in the authority's decision taking. Ruling Chambers take decisions, only subject to review by the administrative courts[56]. In order to execute its duties, the RegTP is vested with far-reaching regulatory and enforcement powers, such as to investigate, to conduct hearings and to seize company documents.

2.6 Special Issues in the Process of Reforms

2.6.1 The Influence of European Law[57]

The EC acts mainly on the basis of the 'Treaty of Rome' of 1957 ('EC Treaty'). It has legislative powers only on those fields for which the EC Treaty specifically establishes such powers. European telecommunication law lies within the wider context of the EC Treaty's overall objective to create a genuine internal market for free movement of people, goods and services, which was introduced in 1987. In 1993, the Maastricht Treaty on EU introduced explicit telecommunication goals: the new Articles 154 to 156 (former Articles 129b to 129d) of the EC Treaty provide for a legal basis for legislative action.

---

[55] All quotations taken from the *RegTP* webpage.

[56] In general legal action against any decision does not suspend its effect.

[57] As main reference for this section see: *Scherer/ Bartsch* (1998) pp. 1 – 7.

The German Postal Reform I was prepared and implemented under the influence[58] of the Commission's 1987 Green Paper on telecommunications[59]. This consultative document introduced a policy for more competition in the telecommunication market combined with a higher degree of harmonisation. In 1990, this dual regulatory approach resulted in two basic acts: the 'Services Directive' and the 'ONP Directive'[60]. The Services Directive[61], based on Art. 90 Para. 3 EC Treaty, served to dismantle monopoly. It provided for the ending of all exclusive rights except for voice telephony, for the separation of regulatory and entrepreneurial functions and for an objective transparent procedure in the admission of new services. The ONP Directive[62], on the other hand, was based on Art. 100a EC Treaty and aimed at the establishment of a system facilitating new entry. Harmonisation was to be achieved by securing open access to network and services.

In the 1993 Council Resolution[63], the Council of Telecommunication Ministers took the landmark decision[64] to liberalise EU voice telephony services by 1998. Liberalisation, harmonisation and support for European providers on the global market have been in the focus of EU policy in this first phase[65]. Very clearly, the process in Germany has been moving along and shaped by decisions and legislative acts of the EU.

---

[58] *Scherer/ Ellinghaus* (1998) p. 135.

[59] *European Commission* (1987).

[60] *Scherer/ Bartsch* (1998) p. 7, for greater detail see pp. 7 – 25.

[61] Commission Directive 90/388/EEC of 28 June 1990 on competition in the markets for telecommunications services, OJ L 192, 24/07/1990; Incorporated by 294A0103(61) (OJ L 001, 03/01/1994); Incorporated by 294A0103(64) (OJ L 001, 03/01/1994); Amended by 394L0046 (OJ L 268, 19/10/1994); Amended by 395L0051 (OJ L 256, 26/10/1995); Amended by 396L0002 (OJ L 020, 26/01/1996); Amended by 396L0019 (OJ L 074, 22/03/1996); Amended by 399L0064 (OJ L 175, 10/07/1999). All EU legislation can be found under http://www.europa.eu.int/eur-lex/index.html

[62] Council Directive 90/387/EEC of 28 June 1990 on the establishment of the internal market for telecommunications services through the implementation of open network provision, OJ L 192, 24/07/1990; Incorporated by 294A0103(61) (OJ L 001, 03/01/1994); Amended by 397L0051 (OJ L 295 29/10/1997).

[63] Council Resolution of 22 July 1993 on the review of the situation in the telecommunication sector and the need for further development in the market (93/C213/01), OJ C 213/1, 06/08/1993.

[64] Final consequence of EU policy and legislation as foreseen by *Baggehufwudt* (1993) p. 179.

[65] *Ordemann* (1997) p. 111.

With the 1997 Green Paper on Convergence[66] and the 1999 Communications Review[67] European telecommunication law entered a new phase[68]. The EU already announced to review the current regulatory framework[69]. Since convergence of different networks, services and terminal equipment will shape future development of telecommunications, information technology and media, sector specific regulation will have to become technological neutral. The new regulatory framework will cover all communication infrastructure and associated services[70]. Having entered the EU legislative process these proposals can be expected to pass as directives within the next two years[71].

2.6.2 The public and academic debate about Liberalisation

State monopoly in German telecommunications had never been seriously questioned until the 1970s when regulatory issues entered discussion from Anglo-Saxon countries. If not for the sake of national military security any more, monopoly was still justified for securing universal services on a high standard, preventing private cherry picking, and dealing with the limitedness of frequencies[72].

Moreover, services via terrestrial networks involving high sunk costs were regarded as natural monopolies. This type of market failure occurs if economies of scale are so great that a tendency towards monopoly seems natural[73] as only one firm can survive in the market. In order to prevent such a monopolist from enjoying supernormal profits public control through nationalised ownership may be justified. Avoiding competitive duplication of networks was thought to

---

66 *European Commission* (1997 b).

67 *European Commission* (1999 b).

68 *Scherer* (2000) pp. 39 – 44.

69 For list of EU secondary legislation in force on information technology, telecommunications and data-processing see: http://www.europa.eu.int/eur-lex/en/lif/reg/en_register_132060.html

70 *European Commission* (1999 b) pp. iv - vi.

71 *Scherer* (2000) p. 36.

72 The Federal Constitution Court (BVerfG) confirmed in 1977: state monopoly does not harm the constitutional 'Right to choose an occupation' as it serves common welfare, *BVerfG* NJW (1978) p. 313.

73 *Griffiths/ Wall* (1996) p. 508.

conserve resources and to minimise overall costs. In general economics this concept was criticised very early by *Demsetz* for it fails to explain the logical link between economies of scale and monopoly price[74]. These thoughts finally elapsed in the theory of contestable markets[75]. It argues that under certain conditions a monopoly may provide services at lowest costs and it will be kept in check by the threat of entry rather than actual entry.

Along with this international debate an increasing academic and political opposition argued against monopoly in Germany. In accordance with the constitutional '*Subsidiaritätsprinzip*'[76] and on the background of the Freiburg School[77] a number of academic studies tried to prove potential benefits from competition[78]. Finally, successful liberalisation in other countries and the process within the EC pressured both sides towards first compromises, which emerged in the Postal Reform I.

After the decision to open the telecommunication market the debate focussed on the separation of posts and telecommunications discussing advantages of combination and of specialisation[79]. Keeping cross-subsidisation from telecommunications in mind, what would be supporting or impeding dynamic development for both entities? Were there any economies of scale or scope? Eventually it was obvious that especially for DBP Telekom more competition required more flexibility. The differences in economic environment had become too great to keep them under one single leadership. Economies of scale and scope were not promising enough to justify the maintenance of such a conglomerate giant.

---

74 *Demsetz* (1968) p. 56.

75 See *Baumol/ Panzar/ Willig* (1988) chap. 7.

76 Translation: Principle of subsidiarity; state activity only in fields where private entrepreneurship does not lead to satisfactory outcome.

77 This ordo-liberal school of thought had a strong belief that an adequate institutional framework combined with free markets is the most decisive parameter for economic success. It was particularly influential in Germany after the Second World War with Franz Böhm and Walter Eucken, intellectual affinity to Friedrich von Hayek and the Austrian School.

78 For example, the Institute of World Economics in Kiel disproved that large investments for construction of modern networks make monopoly inevitable. For higher efficiency the Monopolies Commission argued for privatisation on service, terminal equipment and certification level because these markets could not add any significant economies of scope.

79 *Heuermann/ Schnöring* (1990) pp. 67 – 77 especially.

A rather public than academic debate accompanied DBP's 1993 decision to reform tariffs on the basis of costs[80]. The subsidisation of local by long distance calls could not be held up in a competitive market. New tariffs were to give more flexibility like the possibility of discounts for business customers.

During the legislative process towards the TKG four main points were under strong discussion[81]: Parliamentary opposition regarded the definition of universal services as too weak and called for higher standards. Government argued that this could act as an entry barrier if any innovative service would have to be offered nation-wide. Secondly, the continuing free use of public ways for installations was heavily opposed by local councils as they tried to defend their supposed rights. Thirdly, there was concern about electric power suppliers' cross-subsidising their expected investments into telecommunications with their monopoly rent[82]. Finally, it was criticised that the existing Federal Cartel Office was not assumed with the duties of the regulatory body. Some, however, even wanted the RegTP to be erected as a Highest Federal Authority without ministry control.

Today's debate has moved on: The question of how to open the local loop to competition is very urgent[83]. Alternative networks will play a key role in this[84]. A debate about state ownership and responsibility can be expected when government shares in DT will eventually drop below 50%[85].

2.6.3 Telecommunication Law in the GDR and the '*Neue Länder*'[86]

In the socialist German Democratic Republic (GDR) telecommunications were the task of Deutsche Post (DP) under control of the Ministry of Posts and

[80] *Herbig* (1996) pp. 8 – 11, for tariff structure see *Deutsche Telekom* (1996) pp. 26 – 27.
[81] *Federal Parliament* (1996).
[82] *Monopolies Commission* (1996 b) pp. 25 – 28.
[83] *Wichert-Nick* (1999).
[84] See *Schmittmann* (1998) p. 5 for cable TV network and Section 3.5.
[85] This will be the case in 2001 if the announced merger with the American VoiceStream plc goes ahead, *Handelsblatt* (25/07/2000) p.1.
[86] As main reference for this section see: *Schnöring/ Szafran* (1994) and *Monopolies Commission* (1991).

Telecommunications. In this central planned economy state monopolies were part of the political system. Development of public telecommunications was not of high priority. Investments amounted only to 1% of all economic investment through the 1970s and 1980s[87]. Important closed user groups developed special networks[88], which were not interconnected, not even with the public network, because of uncoordinated construction and technology. Under party dictatorship individual communication was undesirable. This resulted in insufficiency in supply and lack of modern technology[89].

With reunification in 1990, DP was merged with DBP just after the Postal Reform I. The Western telecommunication law and political structure was applied in the East with the exception that monopoly for terminal equipment was to last until 1992 in the *Neue Länder*[90]. Under the political aim for harmonisation of living conditions, existing infrastructure appeared as a bottleneck. Short-term extension of capacity was urgent for prosperous economic development. DBP Telekom tried to speed-up this process investing DM 55 bn into its development program '*Telekom 2000*'[91]. DBP Telekom fully achieved same quality and met all demand (including waiting list) by 1995[92]. For acceleration DBP relied successfully on private operators planning and establishing network segments within the 'Turn-Key Project'. Also licences for GSM mobile phone networks awarded to DBP Telekom and Mannesmann in 1990 were extended to the territories of the *Neue Länder* in 1991.

---

[87] In West Germany, DBP could invest 3–4% of all economic investment, *Schnöring/Szafran* (1994) p.10.

[88] By 1989, 23 special networks for armed forces, State Security Service, administration and certain industries.

[89] See table and figures in Appendix 6.

[90] *Monopolies Commission* (1991) pp. 16 – 17.

[91] *Monopolies Commission* (1991) pp. 14 – 16. The program involved 7.2 m new main lines, 300,000 mobile phone accesses, 68,000 new public phone boxes, and 2.2 m cable TV accesses.

[92] *Deutsche Telekom* (1996) p. 14.

3 The Market for Landlines Telecommunications

3.1 Background for Analysis

The following chapter will provide an analysis of the market structure of landline telecommunications in Germany and how it has developed since complete liberalisation on 1 January 1998.

3.1.1 The relevant Market

In order to distinguish particular markets the concept of 'relevant markets' can be employed from competition law, where clear borderlines between markets are essential[93]. Markets can be differentiated with respect to time, geography and product.

The market of landlines is characterised by temporal market factors of continuous line rental to acquire services punctually for a certain length in time. Geographically the relevant market covers the territory of the Federal Republic of Germany[94]. For defining the relevant product market the most important factor is substitutability[95] of either supply ('industry concept') or demand ('product concept'). The industry concept points at technical ways of access and levels of production[96]. Landlines are distinctive in the technical way they transmit data through closed cable networks in more than one direction. The product concept considers goods and services of similar price and quality, which

---

[93] *Furse* (1999) pp. 188 – 197, which refers to jurisdiction of European Court of Justice (ECJ) on *United Brands Co.* v *Commission*, case 27/76 [1978] 1 CMLR 429. For similar approaches in economic theory see *Auerbach* (1988) pp. 34 – 38.

[94] As given in the licences under Sec. 6 TKG.

[95] As it is often employed by the ECJ, *Furse* (1999) p. 189: the economic equivalent concept would be cross-elasticities of demand, *Stead/ Curwen/ Lawler* (1996) pp. 25 – 26.

[96] *Merkin/ Williams* (1984) p. 143, *Wichert-Nick* (1999) p. 24.

satisfy the same needs, as one market[97]. Landline networks can offer high quality and capacity at relatively low prices. Even though there may be threat of substitution and a process of convergence, so far landlines can be regarded as one distinct relevant market.

Since the mid 1990s the German market for landlines can also be assumed as homogenous between former East and West Germany after quality and number of main lines accesses had reached Western standard[98]. Purchasing power and communication habits are assimilating at a slower pace.

3.1.2 Overview over Market Analysis

The market analysis will follow *Porter*'s 'Five Forces' approach[99], which he introduced as a means of examining the competitive environment at the level of strategic business units[100].

Figure 3.1: *Porter*'s 'Five Forces'

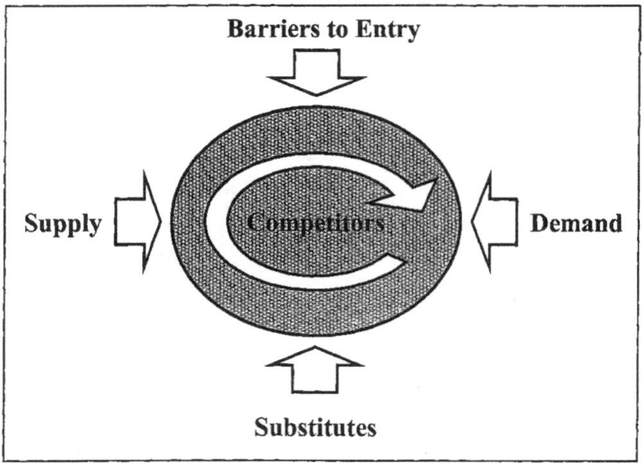

97 *Merkin/ Williams* (1984) pp. 136 – 139, *Wichert-Nick* (1999) p. 25 calls it 'substitution concept'.
98 *Herbig* (1996) p. 8, see also Appendix 6 Figure A6.1.
99 *Porter* (1980) pp. 3 – 5.
100 *Johnson/ Scholes* (1997) p. 108.

Five key forces with strong interrelations have shaped the market for landlines telecommunications: barriers to entry, supply with information technology, demand for telecommunications, threats from substitutes and, finally, competitors within the market.

It is important to emphasise that *Porter* developed his approach in the late 1970s in order to recommend future strategies within a very static industrial environment. Even though telecommunications has obviously been one of the most rapidly changing industries over the last decade, the 'Five Forces' can still be used as a structured framework to examine development from *past* to *present*. With regard to fundamental changes in the past this analysis can rely on true data and facts of industrial structure, rather than predictions.

3.2 Barriers to Entry

With liberalisation barriers to entry have come down dramatically. Despite of several different definitions for such in economic literature, all agree on their attention on different opportunities facing insiders and outsiders of the market[101]. *Bain* identified three categories of barriers, namely barriers upon legislation and rights, upon customers' preference and upon economies of scale[102].

3.2.1 Market Legislation and Network Control

Legislative barriers of entry changed from monopoly to a regulated market as described in Chapter 2 with regulation required until DT's dominance is controlled sufficiently by competition. To prevent DT from erecting new barriers by limit pricing all tariffs have to be approved *ex ante* by the RegTP[103].

As the existing landline network remained under DT ownership it is necessary to secure fair and equal access for competitors. For fair competition

101 *Demsetz* (1982) p. 48.
102 *Bain* (1972) pp. 98, 82 – 83.
103 An *Analytical cost model* is used, outlined under http://www.regtp.de/en/costmodel/start/fs_12.html

regulation involved fixed preservice charges for interconnection, carrier services and unbundled access to the local loop[104]. Obviously the market reacts very sensitively to these prices as they encourage or discourage network investment and competition.

3.2.2 Preference and Brand Loyalty of Customers

Preference and brand loyalty of customers to which firms react with product differentiation determine the eventual success in the market. In times of state monopoly customers obviously did not have any choice and were hence valued rather as *users* than as *customers*. As early as 1994 in preparation for privatisation DT tried to shift its image from being a technology orientated monopolist to a caring and dynamic competitor. New cost based tariffs introduced in 1996 followed a clear segmentation of business and residential customer groups for special needs.

With entry of competitors this process gained momentum. Competitors are fighting for distinguished market positions, which involves advertising and often tariffs with at least one price cherry. But customers confronted with multiple new suppliers with well over a hundred different tariffs soon lost track in the 'tariff jungle' and their decisions have become less rational. Especially for business customers not only price, but also reliability, quality and customer service have become decisive elements.

Overall brand loyalty crumbled very fast in the early stages of competition as customers gained trust in new competitors. After one year already 1/6 of all customers had used one of the new providers[105].

3.2.3 Economies of Scale and Scope

Economies of scale deter entry by forcing the entrant to come in at large scale and risk strong reactions or at small scale and face cost disadvantages[106]. Due to

---

[104] For detail see Section 5.3 on Regulation at work.
[105] *RegTP* (1999 a) p. 8.
[106] *Porter* (1980) p. 7.

high irreversible construction and running costs and the indivisibility of terrestrial networks, landlines telecommunications had long been regarded as a natural monopoly.

However, past experience suggests that competitive supply becomes possible as economies of scale vary over time. Scale economies may be reached relatively early in long-distance transmission, leaving the residual cost advantage from a larger system as relatively small compared with possible dynamic efficiency gains. Lifecycle effects let terrestrial networks pass through three stages[107]:

- Building critical mass: Initially network externality favours a single, unified structure.
- Cross-subsidy: With continuing growth internal dynamics begin to benefit some users at the expense of others.
- Pluralistic structure: Weakening scale economies and diverting interests cause structure to convert into interconnected, but multiple ownership networks.

Interconnection technology made utilisation of telecommunication lines by more than one firm possible and has increased efficiency in exploitation. Therefore, it is no longer necessary to connect every single household to offer a new nation-wide service. This has dropped economies of scale considerably for long-distance calls. Economies of scale in modern telecommunications at all levels are not so much a matter of size, but to what extent the technology applied can secure increasing usage and optimal exploitation of capacity[108].

Economies of scope exist where offering a variety of goods and services help competitors to lower their average costs. Since the present network can transmit data of any kind, economies of scope occur with converging services beyond telephony. Most promising are services involving data transfers like banking, Internet usage and e-commerce. Therefore, most companies operating

---

[107] Theory of *Network Tipping* by E. M. Noam, taken from *Wheatley* (1999) p. 146.
[108] *Wheatley* (1999) p. 122 and *Burr* (1995) pp. 102 – 107.

landlines networks offer Internet access and portals and have invested in Internet based services[109].

3.3 Structure of Supply

Information technology supplies equipment to the market to build and run the network. Since the early 1980s Germany has been the strongest European investor in telecommunications and a leading market for telecom technology, even enforced by the development program for the *Neue Länder*.

Table 3.1: Gross investments in telecommunication services (€ bn)[110]

	1980	1985	1988	1990	1992	1993	1998*
Germany	3.9	7.1	8.2	9.4	13.9	13.2	7.9
U.K.	2.0	3.4	4.4	3.7	2.9	3.5	7.3
Euro 12 [111]	14.9	23.0	26.8	32.2	34.3	36.4	31.5

Note: * Data from *RegTP* (1999 b) p. 109 and *Siemens* (2000) pp. 58 – 59. Data for Euro 12 only include incumbent operators except for Germany and the U.K.

This put Germany and hence DT in a position where it cannot only rely on modern network technology, but also on a well-trained workforce and domestic companies with long experience in production and innovation.

3.3.1 Network Architecture

The network architecture consists of three hierarchical networks: local, national or domestic and international, as shown in Figure 3.2. Interconnection with other networks, like mobile phones, is possible on every level. Due to high

[109] DT's Internet subsidiary T-Online is at present Europe's largest Internet provider with 6 m customers including the French branch Club Internet, *Deutsche Telekom* (2000 b) p. 3. DT also holds a 21.4% share in comdirect, the Internet banking branch of Commerzbank.

[110] Source: *European Commission* (1997 a) p. 26-21.

[111] Euro 12: Belgium, Denmark, France, Germany, Greece, Ireland, Italy, Luxembourg, Netherlands, Portugal, Spain and U.K.

requirements of technology and construction work, building the local network makes up for 70 – 80% of all network-related investments[112]. This architecture mainly originates from the historical way the network was established.

Figure 3.2: Traditional Network architecture[113]

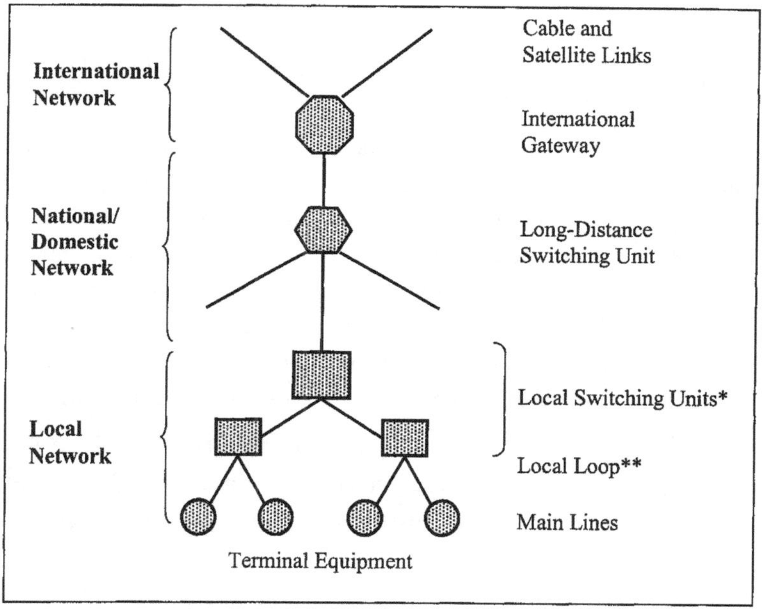

Note: * Switching units operate on various levels.
** Distance between Main Lines and Local Switching Units (Local Loop) is app. 2 km.

Additional digital *local*, *wide* and *metropolitan area networks* (LAN, WAN, MAN) have been established especially for business data transfer. Data traffic often only needs one way and can be delivered in packets, but requires highly variable channel capacity. Corresponding protocols set formats and procedures and govern the exact form of transmission. One developed for high-speed transmission is the *Asynchronous Transfer Mode* (ATM). Another one

112 *Wichert-Nick* (1999) p. 27.
113 Figure based on *Wichert-Nick* (1999) p. 27 and *Wheatley* (1999) p. 42.

widely used in public networks is the *Internet Protocol* (IP), which includes error-detection and correction procedures[114].

3.3.2 Terminal Equipment Technology

Recent trends in terminal equipment technology are digitisation, data compression and diversification[115].

In the past all telecommunications was analogue. With digital transmission, the analogue wave is replaced by binary codes allowing for carriage of any kind of data along the same network. Moreover, digitisation is a requirement for full data compression where sending equipment is used to reduce the amount of data. This allows for transmission of large files and moving pictures. Advantages of digitisation and data compression are more efficient and hence less expensive use of transmission media, better quality and transmission of different kind of information (voice, video, files) over the same network.

Terminal equipment has become very diversified and specialised in soft- and hardware. Advancing standardisation allows increasing global economies of scale to producers, which strengthens their bargaining power against network providers.

3.3.3 Network Technology

Transmission capacity allowing flexibility through sufficient speed and bandwidth is the technological factor for success in telecommunications[116]. Capacity is determined by network technology, which consists of transmission media and switching units.

The entire German network was already digitised under monopoly by 1997[117]. The main transmission media still is copper due to its use in the local loop. But today's supply is characterised by diversification. In Germany, the

[114] *Wheatley* (1999) pp. 44 – 45, 47.
[115] See *Wheatley* (1999) pp. 32 – 36, 46 – 46 and *Wichert-Nick* (1999) pp. 28 – 29.
[116] Falk Janotta, Head of IT, in *Mobilcom* (2000) p. 20.
[117] *Deutsche Telekom* (1998) p. 27 and (1996) p. 14.

whole national and international network as well as some local loops now relies on optical fibre and satellite technology.

Table 3.2: Copper and Optical Fibre in DT Network 1990 – 1999 (1,000 km)[118]

	1990	1992	1994	1996	1997	1998	1999
Copper	1,309.7	1,204.1	1,399.9	1,446.1	1,455.7	1,452.3	1,450.2
Optical Fibre	40.0	67.2	114.7	137.6	150.6	157.4	162.5

Note: In 1999 competitors owned optical fibre networks of 70,000 km in length[119].

For cable TV in local networks coaxial cables are used. The wireless local loop (WLL) is on its way since frequencies were first given out in April 1999[120]. This technology may be crucial for competition within the local network to bypass DT's local network[121]. Transmission media mainly differ in the range of frequencies carried, which is called the bandwidth[122], and thus their cost structure.

Table 3.3: Network technology in comparison[123]

	Recent Technology (Telephony and Internet separate)	**New/ Future Technology** (Telephony and Internet combined)	**Advantages**
Technology	TDM Time Division Multiplexing	ATM / MPLS Multi Protocol Label Switching	Guaranteed quality even with delays / stability
Transmission Technique	SDH Synchrone Data Hierarchy (light on / light off)	D-WDM Dense Wave-length Division Multiplexing (Laser with various colours)	Optimum exploitation of optical fibres
Transmission Costs			Reduction by 90%

118 *Deutsche Telekom* (2000 a) Section Statistical Data. http://www.telekom.de/english/company/inv_rel/ gesch_zahlen/statistik/index.htm

119 *RegTP* (1999 b) p. 116.

120 *RegTP* (1999 a) p. 26.

121 As DT's competitors have recognised: *Mobilcom* (2000) p. 14, *ViagInterkom* (2000) web page.

122 See in detail Section 3.5.

123 Based on *Mobilcom* (2000) p. 17. Note: even recent technology has only been in use since 1998.

For long switching units have used circuit-switching technology, which connects lines end to end for the duration of a call. Modern packet switching splits up information into packets and may send them via different lines for optimal capacity exploitation. Since delays in transmission of packets can occur this technology is mainly employed for data traffic, like the Internet. Wavelength-division multiplexing[124] has the theoretical ability to increase capacity of optical fibre by a factor of 10,000.

Due to high construction costs, narrowband local loops have been a bottleneck for full technical development[125]. Capacity of copper can be increased for broadband technology with *Digital Subscriber Loop* (DSL) systems. Extension of digital transmission beyond the local switching unit permits the development of an *Integrated Services Digital Network* (ISDN). This enables customers to transmit both speech and data over the same cable without the need for special equipment to convert digital signals into analogue form. Other varieties of DSL are *asymmetric* (ADSL), *high-speed* (HDSL) and *very-high-rate* (VDSL) systems, which allow higher exchange rates[126]. DT has been very successful in marketing ISDN in Germany so that half of Western European present accesses are in Germany.

Table 3.4: ISDN accesses, no. of basic rate access connections 1997 – 1999[127]

Basic Rate Access Connections (thousands)	1997	1998	1999
Germany	2,845	4,036	5,272
U.K.	285	350	450
Western Europe	4,834	7,656	10,610
U.S.	1,273	1,713	2,227
Japan	1,947	2,625	4,590

[124] The time between the transmission of consecutive samples in a particular digital channel can be filled with samples from other channels, where cable capacity is used for a large number of different frequency channels simultaneously, *Wheatley* (1999) pp. 34 – 36.

[125] Copper local loops were renewed in 1980's in West and in 1990's in former East Germany, http://www.telekom.de/untern/inv_relations/analyst/index.htm

[126] Exchange rates of more than 64 kbit/s, for broadband 155 Mbit/s seem to become the desirable standard, *Wheatley* (1999) pp. 36 – 37, 45 – 46.

[127] Source: *Siemens* (2000) p. 46.

In 1999 DT began to install ADSL technology in their network and plan to cover half of all German households by the end of 2000[128].

Most of the global equipment supply industry has always been privately owned. It is large ($ 100 bn in 1995) and diverse, but highly concentrated[129]. Companies tend to specialise and powerful economies of scale exist particularly in manufacturing of switching units due to high costs for research and development.

3.3.4 Technologies for the Future

The German public telecommunication network is entering a transition stage from circuit switched to converged networks. Today's still separate networks for voice/ ISDN, Internet and broadband communication will move even closer together in the future[130]. So-called Internet telephony promises to transmit voice over the IP, where every call is charged as a local call to the Internet network and distance becomes irrelevant. Technical problems include interruptions and delays in transfer as voice is split up into packages and missing standardisation so far.

Economic growth depends fundamentally on technological advances in capacity and speed. A new generation of switching systems for integrated voice/ data services will be an important element to stimulate growth[131]. Technological progress is likely to be provided by innovations in electronics, which still seem to follow *Moore's Law*[132]. It can, therefore, be expected that the technology described above will be outdated within the next two to three years.

---

128 *Deutsche Telekom* (2000 b) p. 81.

129 *Wheatley* (1999) p. 66 – 69: in 1993 world-wide only 7 companies accounted for sales of $ 70 bn.

130 For the phenomenon of convergence see Section 3.5.1 for more detail.

131 *Siemens* (2000) p. 12.

132 G. E. Moore: The amount of information storable on a given amount of silicon chip will continue to double every three years, *Wheatley* (1999) p. 55.

3.4 Structure of Demand

Customers' demand has become increasingly aware of communication opportunities. Only within a few years the sector has undergone a considerable cultural change from an approach based essentially on technology to a more commercial approach centred around the customer[133]. Customers are changing their demands from uniform telecommunications to individual multimedia solutions. Operators thus have to adapt their structure so that they can respond appropriately to each category of customer.

3.4.1 Decline in Prices

Figure 3.3: Minimum prices for long-distance calls in the fixed network[134]

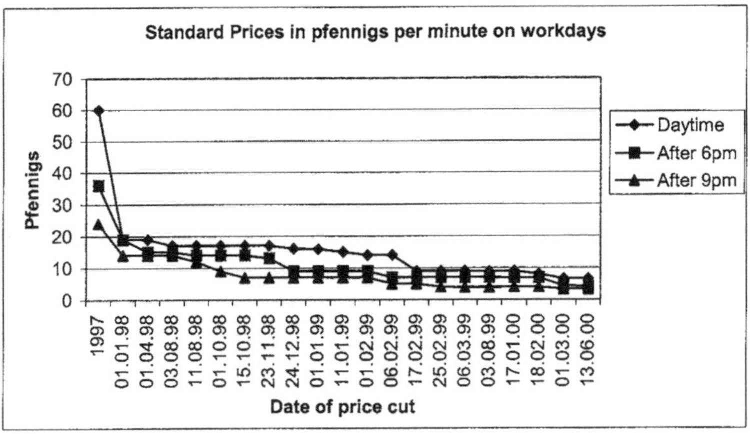

Note: Call-by-call only.

As Figure 3.3 clearly shows, the first thirty months of competition have witnessed an enormous drop in prices, especially for domestic long-distance, Internet, international, and fixed to mobile calls. Now, depending on the time of

[133] *European Commission* (1997 a) p. 26-24.

[134] Figure from *RegTP* (2000 b) p. 18, values on 13/06/00: Daytime 6.6 Pf, After 6pm 4.2 Pf, After 9pm 3.3 Pf.

day, customers pay anything up to 89% less for a long-distance call on a weekday. Just during the first half of 2000 call-by-call prices fell by up to 40%. Even lower prices are available to customers opting for registered call-by-call, preselection, or direct access packages[135].

For international calls prices have plummeted even more dramatically as shown by the following diagram.

Figure 3.4: Minimum prices for international calls to major destinations[136]

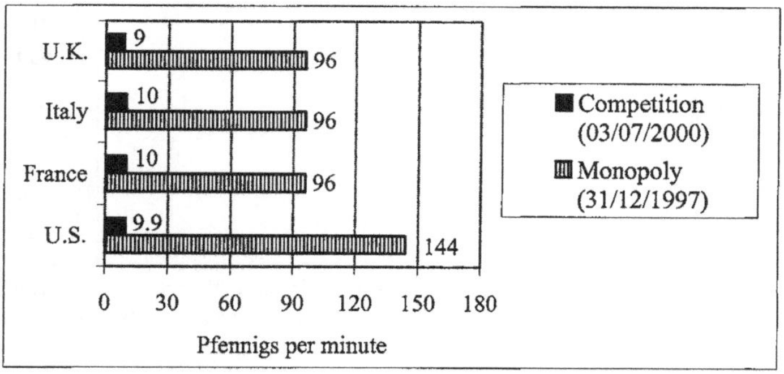

3.4.2 Growth in Sales

Table 3.5 shows the effect of this price development for the landline network market: Despite growing demand for call minutes (17%) and numbers of main lines (4%) revenue from fixed lines services has dropped significantly (9%) in 1999. Revenues for 2000 are expected to remain stable at the 1999 level as the fall in prices since the beginning of the year will be mostly offset by a continued rise in both lines and volume.

Mobile telephony has become the main driver for overall market growth leaving fixed lines revenues in 1999 below 50% of the overall market for the first time. Increase in carrier business results from rise in interconnection and local loop agreements.

135 *RegTP* (2000 b) pp. 17 – 18.
136 *RegTP* (2000 b) p. 19.

Table 3.5: The market for telecommunication services[137]

	1997	1998	1999
Fixed lines call minutes (bn per year)	**178.1**	**196.8**	**231.0**
No. of main lines (m)	45.3	47.0	48.7
Penetration (main lines per 100 habitants)	55.3	57.3	59.3
Total Market Revenue* (bn DM)		86.4	95.5
- Fixed lines services		**45.8**	**41.9**
- Mobile telephony		18.6	24.9
- Leased Lines		2.1	2.1
- Carrier services		3.5	7.1
- Cable TV		4.5	4.6
- Other services**		11.9	14.9

Note: * Excluding invoicing for other companies, internal revenue, and revenue from international interconnect services (included under carrier services in the RegTP's 1998/1999 report on activities).

** For example, data services, Internet access, carriers' revenues from equipment, telephone directories, other radiocommunication services (e.g. broadcast transmitters, satellite services).

3.4.3 Influence of the Internet

With 15% of everyday call volume Internet calls have a significant influence on future demand. Internet use is becoming increasingly popular in business and leisure.

Parallel to development in telephony, decisive to growth in user numbers is not least the increasing range of services available to customers on a call-by-call basis, particularly attractive to newcomers to the Internet. Only during 2000 costs of Internet calls have dropped by 35%. A new low-cost option is direct Internet access at all-inclusive flat rates with monthly charges now between DM 77.00 and 50.00. Also prices for equipment like PC and mobile phones experience a constant decline.

[137] *RegTP* (2000 b) pp. 8, 13, *Siemens* (2000) pp. 28 – 29.

Figure 3.5: Numbers of Internet users in Germany, the U.K. and the U.S.[138]

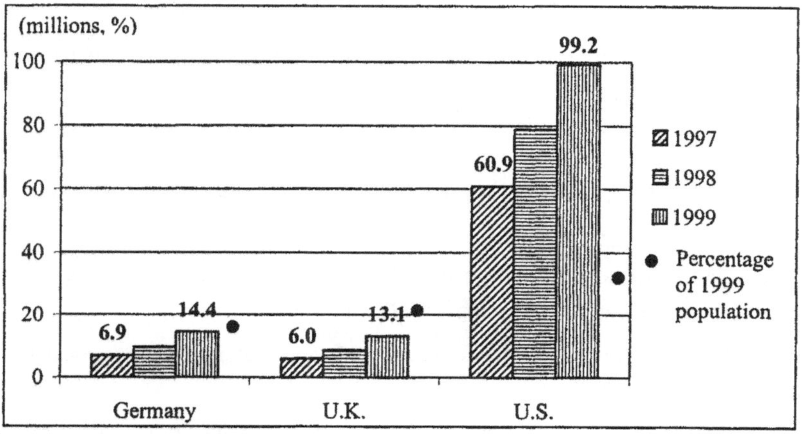

Numerically, the German population has become the largest user group in Europe, but, as shown in Figure 3.5, there is still considerable potential for growth in terms of per capita use. A factor of uncertainty is the matter of regulation for the Internet, which could affect its growth. Further growth is expected from booming e-commerce. With dropping prices and evolving technology Internet use may become an even stronger driving force for fixed network services.

3.4.4 Product Differentiation towards Services

Future development is unlikely to sustain the decline in prices observed so far. Development will shift towards differentiated services. In the past process customers have been offered different modes of access to networks: open or registered call-by-call, preselection or direct access. Flat rate price models will probably be introduced soon for telephony. On this basis evolution will continue, especially for large and small businesses, offering all-inclusive multimedia solutions. More generally, tariffs will move away from charging per time to charging per data quantity[139].

---

[138] *RegTP* (2000 b) p. 25, *Siemens* (2000) p. 49.
[139] *Hüschl Rautenberg* (2000) pp. 81 – 84.

3.5 Threats from Substitutes

The market of landline telecommunications is threatened by various substitutes due to a process of convergence in the broader industry.

3.5.1 Convergence in the Information Industry

Convergence in the information industry has been discussed for long and has lead to the European Commission's 1997 Green Paper.

> "The term convergence eludes precise definition, but it is most commonly expressed as:
>
> - the ability of different network platforms to carry essentially similar kinds of services, or
> - the coming together of consumer devices such as the telephone, television and personal computer"[140].

The phenomenon of convergence attempts to analyse how telecommunications, media and IT companies are using the flexibility of digital technologies to offer services outside their traditional business sectors, increasingly on an international or global scale. Convergence proceeds simultaneously on different stages:

Figure 3.6: Stages of Convergence[141]

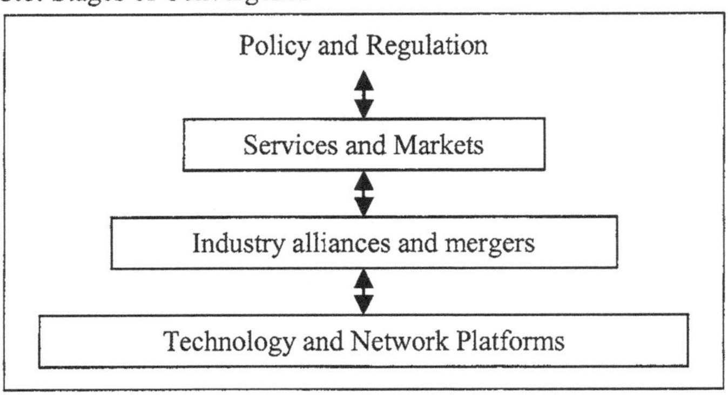

[140] *European Commission* (1997 b) chap. I.1.

[141] Taken from *European Commission* (1997 b) chap. I.1.

Traditionally, communication media were separate and offered distinct services. They operated on different networks, used different equipment and were regulated by different laws and regulators. Nowadays digital technology allows a substantially higher capacity of traditional and new services to be transported over the same networks and to use integrated consumer devices for purposes such as telephony, television or personal computing. Convergence can be observed at terminal equipment, network and service level. Figure 3.7 shows these levels as three concentric circles.

Figure 3.7: Convergence in the Information Industry[142]

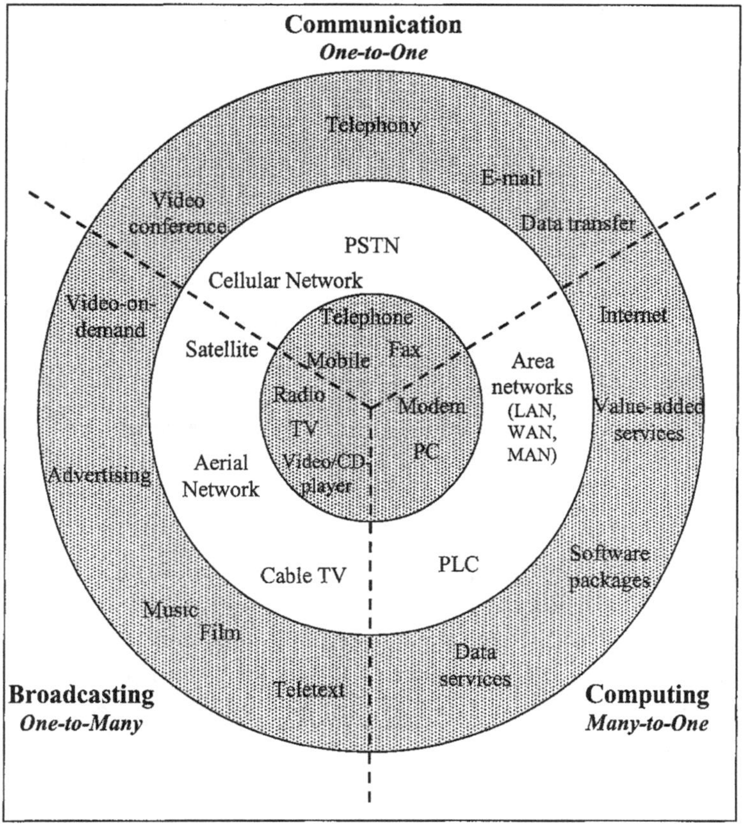

[142] Developed from *Mahrdt* (1998) p. 47.

3.5.2 Cellular Mobile Communications Networks

The late 1990s saw a lasting boom in mobile telecommunications in Germany with mobile subscriptions eating into the fixed line business. Cellular mobile technology divides a territory into cells, each of which is served by a base station. With low transmission power within these cells allocated frequencies can be reused in different cells. Intelligent technology is needed to handover calls when moving from one cell into another. In Germany the first analogue C-network was launched in 1986, but will only be operating until December 2000. Four digital networks of the so-called second generation are operating in Germany based on GSM technology.

Table 3.6: Digital Mobile Networks in Germany[143]

	D1 T-Mobil	D2 Mannesmann	E1 E-plus	E2 ViagInterkom
Operating since	1992	1992	1994	1998
Ownership	DT 100%	Vodafone100%	KPN 77.5% Bell South 22.5%	e.on* 45% BT 45% Telenor 10%
Customer share	39.4%	40.6%	14.7%	5.3%
Landline Network	DT	Arcor, Otelo	None	ViagInterkom

Note: * e.on, the electricity supplier formerly called Viag, announced after the UMTS auction to sell its shares to BT.

Fierce competition in digital networks from the beginning resulted in steady improvements in quality, early full coverage and constant decline in prices. The success is expressed in high growth rates. Density of mobile phones is expected to overtake fixed main lines by early 2001 at the latest since growth in customer numbers in the first six months of 2000 has exceeded all expectations[144].

---

[143] Sources: *RegTP* (2000 b) p. 20, *Siemens* (2000) p. 9, *Wichert-Nick* (1999) p. 37.

[144] *RegTP* (2000 b) pp. 19 – 20, by end of June 2000 number of customers was 34.1 m giving a penetration rate of 41.6%.

Figure 3.8: Development in Mobile Subscription[145]

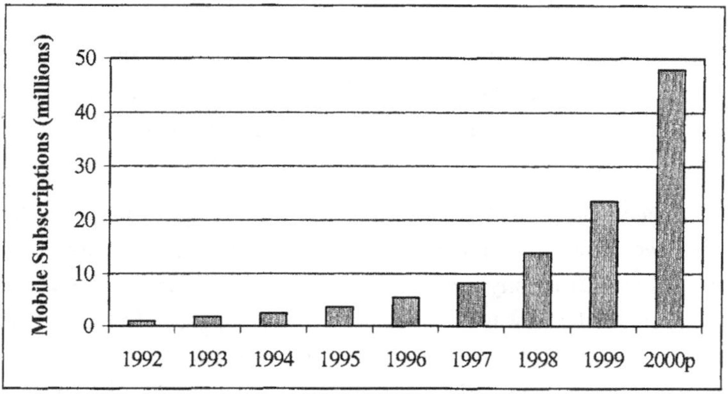

Note: Mobile data include subscription to analogue C-network, app. 100,000 at present, which DT will take out of operation on 31 December 2000.

Present GSM technology only allows for limited data transmission by WAP-Services. New UMTS technology will enable complete mobile Internet access and moving pictures transmission. For market launch in Germany in 2002, six licences were sold in August 2000 for an overall of DM 99.36 bn. In addition to the existing digital networks two companies were successful: Mobilcom (partnership with France Télécom) and 3G (Telefónica and Sonera). As Internet usage is the strong driver of growth in landlines traffic this will put high pressure on growth in landlines transmission. Since payment and data transfer from mobile handsets are safer and more convenient than using a PC, m-commerce (trade via mobile access to the Internet) is expected to develop much faster than e-commerce.

However, there are uncertainties involved. Upgrade for UMTS requires high investment not only for licences in different countries, but also for network and handset technology. This may raise operating costs above GSM level and hinder future growth. Only if an adequate level of prices and quality can be achieved, mobile communications will develop from a complementary technology to a full substitute[146].

---

145 Sources: *RegTP* (2000 b) p. 20. For 2000 values are predicted.

146 *Monopolies Commission* (1999) No. 9.

3.5.3 Satellite Communications Networks

Satellite systems can transmit broadband signals over long distances. About 30% of German households receive their TV programs via satellite and international telecommunications especially across the Atlantic uses this system. Satellite services include *global positioning systems* (GPS).

Desire for global mobility and broadband services gave idea to establish worldwide telecommunication networks based on satellite technology. Satellites can pick up signals from any remote place on the Earth's surface and transmit the call to terrestrial gateways where the signal is handed over into landline networks. To avoid delays in transmission multiple satellites orbit less than 1,500 km above the ground (LEO). This technology, however, suffers from high entry costs since any satellite launch adds substantial costs with high risk of complete failure. Table 3.7 shows data of two satellite networks, one of which, however, went bankrupt as early as May 2000.

Table 3.7: Global Satellite Telecommunications Networks at a glance[147]

	'Iridium'	*'Globalstar'*
No. of satellites	66+6 spare	48+8 spare
Earth coverage	100%	80% after rollout
Start of Operation	1998 out of work in May 2000	late 1999
Investment ($ bn)	5	1.8
Main shareholder	Motorola	Loral
Services	speech, data, paging	speech, (data not before 2001)
Subscriptions	55,000	67,000

Satellite Internet access has been offered in Germany by a handful of companies since mid-1999. Only since the beginning of 2000, data can be

[147] Company data taken from web pages http://www.iridium.com and http://www.globalstar.com and *Wheatley* (1999) pp. 76 – 77.

transmitted in both directions via a *Eutelsat* satellite[148]. This access option is targeted chiefly at business customers.

3.5.4 Cable TV Networks

Cable TV networks using coaxial wires can be upgraded with fibre feeders and a return channel for interactive multimedia services. The successful introduction of Internet access via modem[149] allows access to broadcast and broadband telecommunication services via cable TV networks.

The German cable TV network is the largest single network (over 20m households) with the highest penetration (58% households)[150] world-wide. It was mainly constructed and hence owned by DT. DT started to split it up into nine regional networks and to sell majority stakes, but keeping 25% + 1 share in each[151]. Due to this structure in ownership networks in other countries have been upgraded much faster. Obviously DT have no urgent interest to develop this network beyond its present use for TV and radio. As long as DT owns considerable shares it will never be a real threat to DT's landlines network. This is why the Monopolies Commission has voted for a complete sale of this network since 1996[152].

Besides the technical feasibility there are a number of uncertainties involved in its economic use: very sensitive costs to penetration, competition of other potential substitutes, and diverse interest groups like shareholders, broadcasting stations and building companies[153].

---

148 *RegTP* (2000 b) pp. 16 – 17.

149 In Germany mainly sold by Met@box, details on technology and future expectations on homepage: http://www.metabox.de/productsdesign/englisch/mbtech_e-f.html

150 *RegTP* (2000 b) p. 16.

151 *Deutsche Telekom* in Information for Business Analysts on 19/04/2000, http://www.telekom.de/untern/inv_relations/analyst/index.htm, so far two networks are partly sold.

152 *Monopolies Commission* (1996 a) p. 28, No. 62 – 64.

153 *Distelkamp* (2000) p. 5.

3.5.5 Electric Power Lines Networks

No network is globally as widespread as electrical power grids. Communication hooked on low voltage electricity, commonly referred to as *powerline communications* (PLC)[154], is technical feasible[155], but faces two major problems[156]: Usage of same frequencies across electric powerlines causes distortion in aerial transmission, but there may not be enough frequencies available. Secondly, transmission costs including additional equipment have to be competitive to be successful in the market. So far PLC technology seems to be not advanced enough for market success.

Looking at the competitive environment in Germany, a launch appears promising within an only very short time period as long as competing technologies like ASDL, WLL and UMTS are not easily available yet. Nevertheless may this technology be of high use in other countries, which are less developed in their telecommunication networks.

3.5.6 Concluding Evaluation

In conclusion, threat from substitutes is, at least for the predictable future, limited as all alternative technologies face technical and economic difficulties in providing the same standard of services as landlines. Mobile telecommunications has proved the greatest challenge to landlines, but the overall market seems to be growing strongly enough to provide complementary growth. Table 3.8 summarises the main characteristics of landlines network and its potential substitutes.

---

154 *RegTP* (2000 a) p. 31.

155 For details in technology see *Ascom* web site: http://www.ascom.ch/plc/int_home.htm

156 *Wirtschaftwoche* (10/02/2000) pp. 127 – 128.

Table 3.8: Characteristics of Networks

	Landlines	**Mobile**	Satellite	CableTV	PLC
Technology	ADSL/WLL	UMTS	LEO	Upgrade	Upgrade
Availability	2000	2002	now	now	?
Speech/data transmission	possible	possible	possible	possible	possible
Initial upgrade costs	low	very high	none	high	low
Transmission speed (Mbit/s)	< 6 / > 0.5*	max. 2	< 4		app. 1
Ratio of fix over variable Costs	high	average	very high	average	low
Ratio of sunk over reversible costs	high	high	very high	average	low
Economies of scale	average	high	very high	average	low
Economies of scope	possible**	possible**	possible	high	v. high***

Note: * Downstream to customer / Upstream into the network.
** With e-/ m-commerce.
*** With electric power supply.

3.6 Structure of Competitors

As barriers of entry changed, number and size of competitors within this growing market have risen dramatically. The following table shows this development:

Table 3.9: Number of licences granted until July 2000[157]

	1996 2nd half	1997	1998	1999	2000 1st half	**Total**
Class 3	14	51	146	154	191	**556**
Class 4	3	39	122	98	59	**321**

157 *RegTP* (2000 b) p. 29.

Since most companies need both class 3 (for transmission paths) and class 4 licences (for voice telephony) for their business these licences are in the possession of only 305 companies, 91 of which are spin-offs from public utilities and municipal plants.

3.6.1 Concentration

Table 3.10: Market shares of incumbent and competitors in 1999[158]

		Deutsche Telekom		Competitors	
		Absolute	Percentage	Absolute	Percentage
Local calls*	Revenue (DM bn)	2.14	**98.2**	0.04	**1.8**
	No. of minutes (bn)	31.40	**97.5**	0.80	**2.5**
Long-distance calls*	Revenue (DM bn)	1.60	**71.4**	0.64	**28.6**
	No. of minutes (bn)	9.90	**64.7**	5.40	**35.3**
International calls*	Revenue (DM bn)	0.82	**69.5**	0.36	**30.5**
	No. of minutes (bn)	1.00	**62.5**	0.60	**37.5**
Overall	Revenue (DM bn)	32.7	**68.0**	9.2	**22.0**
	No. of minutes (bn)	189.0	**81.8**	42.0	**18.2**
Main lines	No. (thousands)	48,190	**99.0**	509	**1.0**

Note: * Values only for first quarter of 1999.

These figures reveal that the market of landline telecommunications is still very concentrated with DT as the major player enjoying 68% of revenues and covering over 80% of demand. The high number of operators indicates high potential for competition in the market rather than the current competitive level.

But concentration is of very different degree in different submarkets. The following table shows the extent to which new entrants are effectively active on them.

---

158 Data from *Monopolies Commission* (1999) No.19, 32, 33, *RegTP* (1999 b) pp. 110 – 113, *RegTP* (2000 b) pp. 8, 13, *Deutsche Telekom* (2000 a) p. 44.

Table 3.11: Percentage of territory/population with choice of operator in 1999[159]

	Local calls		Long-distance calls		International calls	
	Territory	Population	Territory	Population	Territory	Population
Germany	**0.4%**	**5%**	100%	100%	100%	100%
U.K.	100%	100%	100%	100%	100%	100%

It emphasises the fact that competition in the local loop is still very undeveloped. Only 5% can choose between more than one operator for local calls. As long as this status lasts DT will remain a widely unchallenged incumbent. But things seem on their way as by June 2000, 82 companies had concluded local loop agreements with DT and alternative technologies are under construction for the local loop. But experience in other countries like the U.S. and U.K. have shown that monopoly in the local loop even if customers do have the choice remains almost unchallenged[160].

Many new entrants initially concentrate on long-distance and international services or business customers. Here scale economies are achieved at an early stage and monopoly prices used to be high to subsidise local calls. Present regulatory framework with fixed rates for interconnection and local loop rental seems to favour this[161]. So far competitors have mainly offered services of high value to keep a high ratio of revenues and costs.

3.6.2 Capitalisation

An important measure of size and indicator for future performance as expected by the financial markets is total market capitalisation. As Figure 3.9 indicates DT is still the giant in the market. Mannesmann is the strongest competitor due to valuable assets in its traditional core businesses tubes, engineering and automotives. In 1999 Mannesmann still generated 60% of total revenues from these sectors. These sectors were sold in the first half of 2000 after the Vodafone

159 Source: *European Commission* (1999 c) pp. 149 – 152.
160 *Monopolies Commission* (1999) No. 58.
161 *Monopolies Commission* (1999) No. 36.

take-over. The British-U.S. Vodafone-Airtouch group is following a mobile focused strategy on global markets. Residual companies in the German market are small, but in 1999 Mannesmann's landlines subsidiary Arcor, together with Mobilcom and Debitel were among the top 20 German companies with respect to increase in revenue[162].

Figure 3.9: Market capitalisation of DT and its main listed competitors[163]

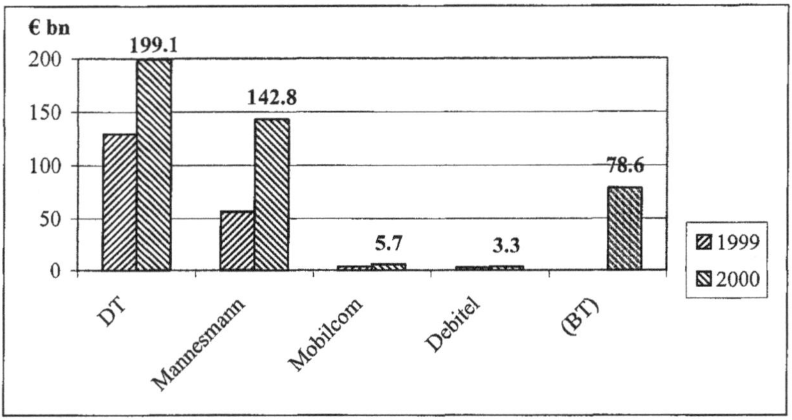

3.6.3 Growth

Competitors do not only grow in absolute terms, but the histograms of Figure 3.10 show growth of competitors share. The overall growth in market volume over the last two years has mainly been generated by DT's competitors. More important is, however, that DT revenue from landlines crumbled due to decline in prices, but suffered stronger than its competitors. But since they had to rely on DT's network for transmission DT has also had a large share in competitors' revenue from carrier payments. Hence DT could increase carrier business by 79% in 1999 to DM 5.7 bn[164].

---

[162] *FAZ* (04/07/2000) p. U1.
[163] *Datastream*, values from Frankfurt XETRA 20/06/2000, for BT 11/09/2000.
[164] *Deutsche Telekom* (2000 a) p. 56.

Figure 3.10: Development in Volume and Revenue 1997 – 1999[165]

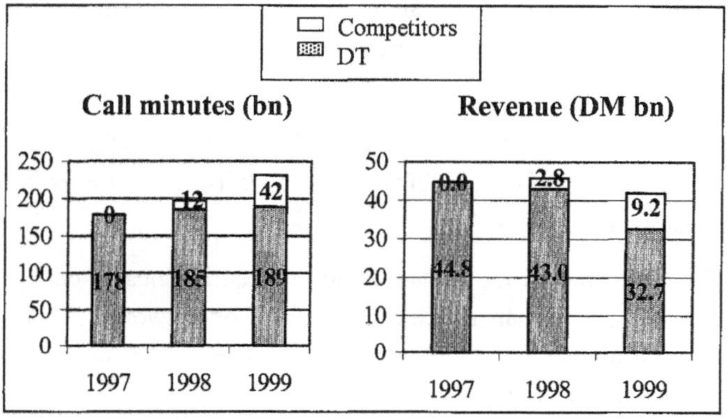

Note: Revenues include revenue from Internet call-by-call services; it cannot be differentiated between charges for lines and Internet use.

3.6.4 Segmentation

As competitors developed from outsiders to insiders of the market, criteria for segmentation changed. At the time of entry it was important what assets from their core businesses they could employ for an initial boost in the market. For today's evaluation of future opportunities the variety of services is the most important criterion for segmentation.

Since profits could not be expected after entry for quite a while and new entry involved high uncertainties all entrants needed strong financial back-ups in their business plans. Thus new competitors came from varied but relatively limited sectors of mainly four groups:

- Entry came from other network businesses, sometimes joined by international telecommunication companies (Viag and BT formed ViagInterkom). Entrants relied on utilities network experience and infrastructure usually including at least backbones for telecommunications and high financial savings.

[165] *RegTP* (2000 b) p. 13, *RegTP* (1999 b) p. 113.

- The second group had been pushed by changes in their inherited markets into telecommunications at an earlier stage (Mannesmann). They used brand name and telecommunication experiences with some sort of network already established.
- Companies of a third sector entered the landline market from retailing (Mobilcom, Debitel) and built on their skills in customer relationship management.
- Finally companies from abroad or non-related businesses entered without any history in German telecommunications or networks (Tele2). Due to lack in infrastructure of network or customers, they faced the greatest difficulties and uncertainties on entry.

The market has already undergone first phases of consolidation with acquisitions between competitors and buy-ins[166]. Competitors have followed different strategies to find success in the market using their initial assets. They can be roughly differentiated into three groups now:

- **Integrated Players** offer full service along the value chain by operating own networks. They act on different markets and networks like landlines, mobile and Internet (DT, ViagInterkom, Mannesmann).
- **Service Providers** operate leased capacity from third party networks to offer a variety of services (Mobilcom, Tele2, Debitel).
- **Focused Players** offer special services and often only in certain regions (AOL for Internet, NetCologne).

3.6.5 Future Expectations and Strategies

Future performance for competitors will depend on evolution in the whole sector industry. Since each group faces specific challenges to which competitors will have to respond appropriately the market can be expected to develop diversely:

[166] Examples for acquisitions: o.tel.o by Mannesmann, Telepassport by Mobilcom, for buy-ins: Debitel by Swisscom (Switzerland) and Mannesmann by Vodafone (U.K.).

- Large integrated players face increasing international competition in Germany. As their own business portfolio will become increasingly complex, they are restructuring into specialised subsidiaries. International growth along a clear strategy is most important for success on the financial markets for acquisitions.

  Small integrated players face the same challenges, but suffer from their sub-critical size. To defend likely domestic and international take-overs they will need a strategy of focussed growth, independently or by means of alliances and mergers.

- Service Providers are affected by declining margins in their business. They will diversify into related businesses like banking or restructure; either to integrated players by acquiring network capacity or to focused players by specialisation[167].

- Focused Players with success in their core business will strengthen their specialisation by rolling-out current business or creating new revenue streams.

3.7 A European and global Perspective

The past years were not only the first for Germany, but for most of Western Europe under full competition. Simultaneously Eastern Europe has opened their economies for foreign investment in preparation for joining the EU. Therefore, most European markets are experiencing a similar process of new entries.

After a period of price-driven competition markets have undergone first rounds of consolidation pressured by international companies from Europe and overseas. Under convergence, growth and high earnings encourage new entry from related multimedia and service industries. The German market has been in the centre of this motion, as liberalisation came very late and offered high growth expectations within Europe's largest economy. Recent auctions for

[167] Good example is Mobilcom who announced to set up their own bank (*Handelsblatt* (04/07/2000) p. 1), started to invest into a fixed line network (*Mobilcom* (2000) p. 13) and bought a UMTS licence in partnership with France Télécom. This company is converting into a large integrated player.

UMTS licences gave a taste of the consolidation ahead as the same five to six players bid in different countries. But future concentration will not halt at European borders, it will include more transatlantic mergers as the U.S. adopt European advanced standardisation.

Thinking global, the real future markets lie elsewhere in Asian countries like Indonesia, India and China. Market entry is still very restricted, but as these economies hope for state-of-the-art technology, first mover advantages will be very rewarding. The large former Japanese monopolist NTT will play a key role in occupying strategic positions.

Especially global strategic planning involves a high number of uncertainties about winning technologies, future substitutes, Internet usage and sustainability of growth. Regional regulation has often proved to be a contradictory mix of fighting for global free trade and protecting domestic industry in home markets at the same time. When these uncertainties will be resolved a new global industry structure will emerge:

- True regional and global players will be formed.
- Large network companies will coexist with asset-light companies.
- Integrated players will acquire small and focused ones.
- Partnerships and joint ventures will explode because of competition between pure and bundled services.

Overall, telecommunications seem to be a market with high opportunities in hand especially for Europe as today's already leading force in mobiles. Telecommunication infrastructure generates new business in services, like in the financial sector. To take full advantage Europe has to keep the high pace on development in her key markets of Germany, France, Italy and the U.K. Telecommunications has given highest advantages to countries when they opened their markets early.

4 From Monopoly to Competition: Deutsche Telekom AG

Transformation into a private law company in 1995 and competition in the core market since 1998 challenged DT in conduct and performance fundamentally.

4.1 Company Conduct

Changes in the company's conduct have speeded up since privatisation as DT was exposed to a highly competitive environment.

4.1.1 Field Organisation

DT inherited its field organisation of DBP Telekom. This structure was designed for subordinate administration rather than sales. For better customer orientation and market presence it was necessary to open new sales outlets and move them to the High Streets. While their number doubled since 1992, more than a third of existing branch offices have been closed for higher efficiency under a flat hierarchy as shown in Table 4.1.

Table 4.1: Number of branch offices and *T-Punkt* sales outlets 1992 – 1999[168]

	1992	1993	1994	1995	1996	1997	1998	1999
Branch offices	121	121	120	118	118	118	118	78
Sales outlets	292	320	354	364	416	455	578	563

[168] Source: *Deutsche Telekom*, http://www.telekom.de/english/company/inv_rel/info/statistik/ index.htm

4.1.2 Employees

Restructuring field organisation obviously affected staff as much as sites as employees had to be trained for new tasks. The focus has been on ensuring staff employability by offering systematic retraining schemes devised on the basis of business and organisational development needs.

Already in 1994 DBP Telekom announced plans for reorganisation involving cuts in employment by 60,000 until the end of 2000. As Figure 4.1 shows this aim was almost achieved in 1999 already. Important to mention that this negative effect on employment has so far been mostly offset by fast growing demand from new competitors who employed 54,000 people between them by the end of 1999[169].

Figure 4.1: DT employees as at end of each year 1993 – 1999 (in thousands)[170]

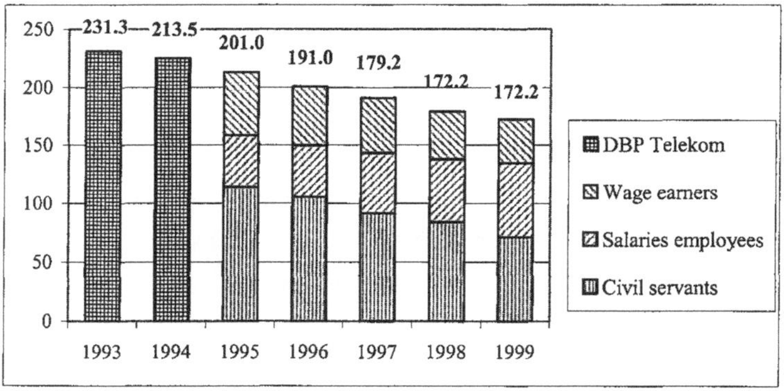

Note: Per end of 1999 DT employed an additional number of 23,555 employees within its acquired subsidiaries like Matav, One2One and Maxmobil.

Focus has not only been on total figures, but just as much on workforce composition as Figure 4.1 indicates. Due to the already mentioned '*Beleihungsmodel*' DT retained all civil servants employed by DBP Telekom. Civil servants still make up for over 40% of DT employees, which cannot be reduced overnight. As these employees kept their status and rights the employment relationship at DT is still directly influenced by public sector pay,

[169] *RegTP* (2000 b) p. 5.
[170] Source: *Deutsche Telekom* (2000 a) p. 27.

pension and career ladder regulations[171]. By extensive use of company agreements with works councils and individuals DT aims to remove chains from its past for full flexibility in its personnel policy.

4.1.3 Structure for Growth

Even though firm size certainly has its advantages it bears risks of slack in efficiency and innovation, especially in very specialised, fast developing areas. Conglomerates tend to slow down in growth and if not restructured will eventually loose market to more flexible competitors.

Figure 4.2: DT's four strategic pillars by the end of 2000[172]

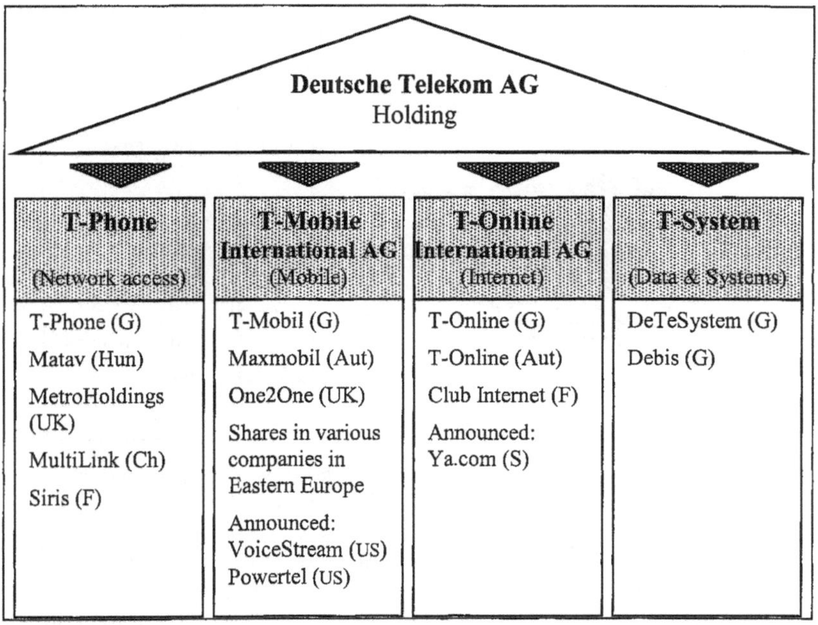

Note: T-Online has been listed since April 2000 with a free float of app. 10%.

[171] *Darbishire* (1997) pp. 214 – 215.
[172] Based on *Managermagazin* (2000), Issue 4, pp. 24 – 30.

To avoid this DT started fundamental restructuring. By the end of 2000 DT will have adopted a new structure, relying on four pillars of distinct core businesses for strategic growth: Network access, mobile communications, online communications, and data communications and systems solutions[173]. Each pillar will focus on its core business with a global perspective for acquisitions and joint ventures. As stock corporations with minority stakes listed, shares can be traded as a currency for growth.

4.1.4 Shareholders

Figure 4.3: DT shareholders per July 2000[174]

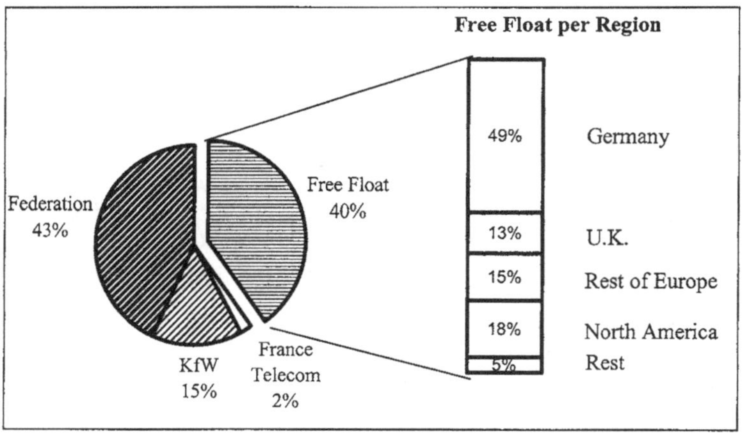

Note: Shares were exchanged with France Telecom as part of partnership program and alliance Global One, which has been resolved.

On the basis of a holding model KfW has taken over federal shares of DT in several tranches between 1997 and 1999. Under this model the German government sells to KfW some of the shares held by the federal republic, purchased at the market price minus a discount. When the shares are later sold on the stock exchange Government obtains a second payment from an upside agreement with KfW. The federal government benefits from KfW's experience in capital market transactions as one of the World's biggest issuer[175].

---

[173] *Deutsche Telekom* (2000 a) p. 1.

[174] Source: *Deutsche Telekom*, http://www.telekom.de/english/company/inv_rel/info/statistik/index.htm

[175] KfW webpage, http://www.kfw.de/e_kfw/beratung/f_beratung11.htm

In three tranches in 1996, 1999 and 2000 numbers of shares have been raised to over 3 bn. DT shares are cross-listed on the Frankfurt and New York stock exchanges to take advantage from international financial markets. In 1996 due to massive advertising the DT share was the first to become a real people's share in Germany spreading share ownership across the population. The 1999 offering was the first ever to offer the same conditions with regards to purchase and allocation to private investors in all Euro-states. After two offerings entirely for capital increase original federal shares were sold in June 2000 by KfW (German Development Bank) for the first time.

Government confirmed its plans to sell all shares eventually at appropriate times. Shareholders structure with a dominant federal share of 58% (including KfW) as shown in Figure 4.3 protects DT from any attempt for hostile take-over. But it also causes two major problems: First it remains, as it has always been, a potential for conflicts between ownership and regulatory interests for Government. Secondly, state majority can prove to be a disadvantage for global acquisitions in foreign markets[176].

4.2 Company Performance

Success of liberalisation is partly judged on the way DT has been performing within a regulated marketplace.

4.2.1 Share price and Capitalisation

First shares of DT were floated on the stock exchange in November 1996 before the German telecommunication market was completely liberalised. From its opening value of € 16.70[177] the share reached its all-time peak on 6 March 2000 at € 103.90 and has dropped to € 46.20 on 1 September since.

---

[176] On the announcement of DT's acquisition of VoiceStream the U.S. Senate drafted legislation prohibiting take-overs by companies with over 25% foreign state ownership, *FAZ* (15/07/2000) p. 14.

[177] Opening value at 32.50 DM on 18 November 1996.

Figure 4.4: DT Share Price 18 November 1996 – 1 September 2000[178]

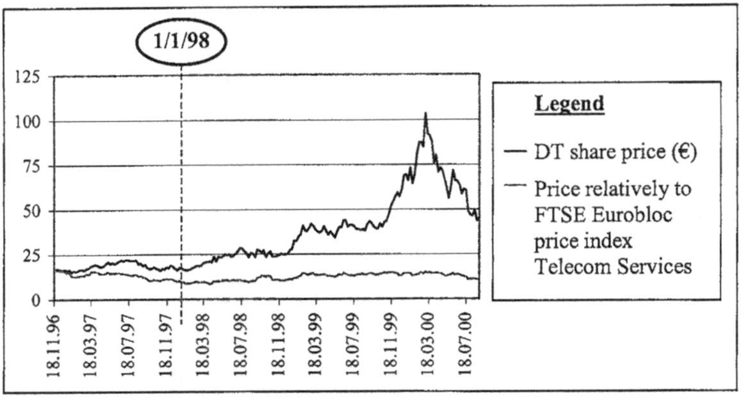

Inspection of Figure 4.4 indicates a value increase by 170% and a performance very much alongside the overall European telecommunications sector. The share has become a heavyweight in the international markets, where its development has proved a good indicator for the whole new economy. This gives the DT share sometimes more attention than desired. Recently share prices suffered from unfulfilled expectations in the general market, high costs for UMTS licences and DT's insufficient internationalisation, which it tried to resolve by two costly American acquisitions of VoiceStream and Powertel.

Due to increases in both number and price of shares market capitalisation of DT has risen from $ 56 bn at the beginning of full competition in January 1998 to $ 180 bn per end of June 2000.

4.2.2 Market and Price Policy

For DT market and price policy has never been without constraints, in the past it was subject to politics, today to regulation. Before new entry was permitted DT had changed its tariff structure for more flexibility, especially to offer discounts to business customers and to lower prices on long-distance calls. These areas were most likely for new entry. The new structure changed from originally two

[178] Source: *Datastream.*

time zones to six referring to four distance zones and halved time units and corresponding prices. As expected emerging competition was price driven. With soon over a dozen competitors with very different tariff structures it became very difficult for customers to work out exact price differences. This confusion helped DT to defend market share. Some companies took advantage themselves, most successful of all Mobilcom offered one price throughout which soon became the early stage benchmark in the price war.

Recognising the importance of transparency DT returned to fewer time zones, but offers more and more special tariffs, following experiences in the mobile market. They are based on trade-offs between line rental and call charges, free calls or inclusive Internet access. With this diversified structure DT tries to be competitive in every customer segment rather than offering one standard tariff only.

4.2.3 Market Share

Figure 4.5: DT market shares per call volume during first Quarter 1999[179]

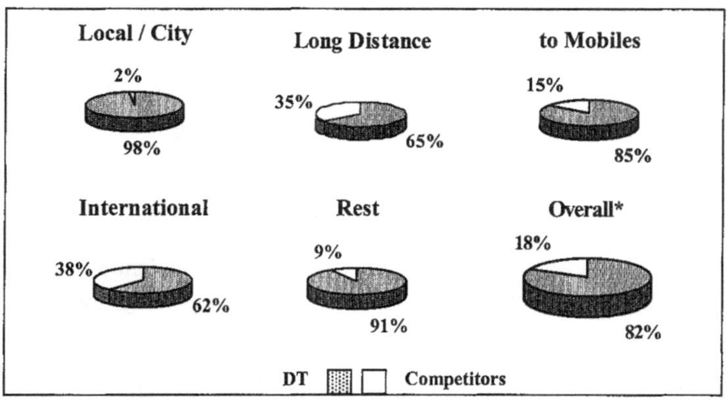

Note: * Overall values represent whole year of 1999.

DT's shares in important submarkets have developed diversely as visualised in Figure 4.5. As mentioned before competitors have been very

[179] Source: see Table 3.10, amended from *RegTP* (1999 b) p. 115.

successful in long-distance, international and connecting mobiles calls where entry was easiest, gaining roughly a third of the market after the first year. Future gains will, however, slow down, as margins in prices are decreasing. But in the local market DT has remained widely unthreatened as a result from high costs in constructing local loops. For sustainable growth direct access to customers will be necessary for competitors.

4.2.4 Growth

Growth has become a core element in DT's strategy. DT has managed to increase net revenues every year since 1995, but composition of sources is shifting. While in 1997 revenues from network communications amounted to € 21.5 bn they dropped by 22% to only € 16.7 bn in 1999[180]. Therefore, in the last year network communications added less than half to DT's total revenues for the first time. This development goes alongside general development in the market[181].

Table 4.2: Revenue, Income and Equity of DT Group at a glance 1995 – 1999[182]

	1995	1996	1997	1998	1999
Net Revenue (€ bn)	30.5	32.3	34.5	35.1	35.5
Net Income (€ bn)	2.7	0.9	1.7	2.2	1.3
Equity Ratio (%)	14.7	25.8	27.5	29.5	35.7

Financially the very low equity ratio was a serious challenge to DT at its birth. It resulted from DBP's costly network development and obligation for pension payments to former and active civil servants. To avoid down ranking of financial markets Government agreed not to sell any shares before 2000. Necessary capital increases in 1996 and 1999 helped improving DT's equity ratio as Table 4.2 indicates.

[180] *Deutsche Telekom* (2000 a) p. 15.

[181] See Table 3.5.

[182] Source: *Deutsche Telekom*, http://www.telekom.de/english/company/inv_rel/gesch_zahlen/statistik/index.htm

4.3 Perspectives for the Future

Since regulation in Germany is aimed at fair competition DT will eventually loose further market share and its role as the only dominant player. For a prosperous future as an independent company DT has not only got to defend its old, but to attack new markets and to launch across the borders. Because of decreasing margins in prices in the home market DT is following a combination of diversification and growth on a global scale. The new company structure with four focused subsidies reveals this strategy.

4.3.1 Diversification and Alliances for new Markets

Independent companies enter strategic alliances in order to achieve mutual aims, like standardisation, market entry, or economies of scope, easier within co-operation[183]. In telecommunications and the wider sector such partnerships have been exploding as a management approach to globalisation and technical progress on multiple levels[184].

Alliances encourage horizontal, vertical or complementary diversification into related services and technology as every partner contributes core skills and assets for overall benefit. DT is part of alliances with computing soft- and hardware and media companies. Especially in the Internet T-Online has set up various alliances with banks and companies to set up virtual marketplaces. Surely T-Mobile will follow with the start of m-commerce.

4.3.2 Global Player for a broad Customer Basis

For long DT regarded the alliance with France Telecom as the cornerstone to its global strategy. Both companies set up joint ventures, most important 'Wind' in Italy and 'Global One', a global high-speed network with the American Sprint. This alliance was abandoned after DT tried to acquire Telecom Italia without its

[183] *Mahrdt* (1998) pp. 49 – 57.
[184] *Mahrdt* (1998) pp. 58 – 75.

partner's approval in May 1999. Now DT is lacking a global partner, a presence in Italy and the Global One-network. After this failure DT decided that

> "Globalisierung heißt für uns: Kontrolle, Akquisition oder Fusion."[185]

Global alliances always bear the risk to interfere with strategies in the future because partners are less free in their decisions and maybe trapped.

Nevertheless, DT is still following a vision of a global player. A fast growing customer basis is vital for survival and independence in a growing market. The global telecommunications landscape is changing quickly due to high acquisition activity and attentions in the stock markets. Compared to its European and U.S. competitors DT managed to improve its position by market capitalisation since complete liberalisation – even without large mergers so far.

Figure 4.6: Top 10 European and U.S. companies by market capitalisation[186]

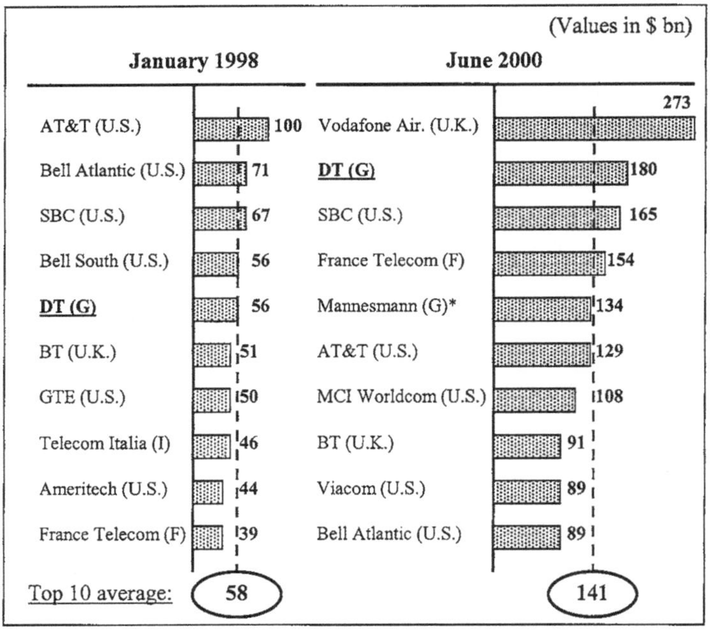

Note: * Vodafone Airtouch acquired Mannesmann in March 2000, which was a conglomerate of engineering and telecommunications.

---

[185] Translation: To us globalisation means: control, acquisition or merger. CEO Dr. Sommer in interview in *Wirtschaftswoche* (13/04/2000) pp. 110 – 111.

[186] Source: *Datastream.*

DT will only hold this position if it can deliver up to the high expectations for global success. So far, as shown in Figure 4.2, DT only has a very limited global standing. Therefore, the financial markets have been expecting the acquisition of a major European and U.S. network based company for long. This would give DT the chance to rely on a global network to serve increasingly important global customers. But at the same time key positions in the Asian-Pacific region have to be occupied. DT is facing strong competitors in the marketplace with Vodafone for European mobiles, AOL for global Internet and European, U.S. and Japanese network companies. To get ahead it is time for action in global acquisitions.

5 Regulation and Deregulation in Telecommunications

5.1 Relationships around the Regulatory Authority (RegTP)

For many problems the TKG does not provide fixed and defined legal solutions. This

> "open approach to problem solving"[187]

hands over a lot of power to the RegTP. Interest groups have formed a complex grid to influence regulation.

Figure 5.1: Interest groups around the RegTP[188]

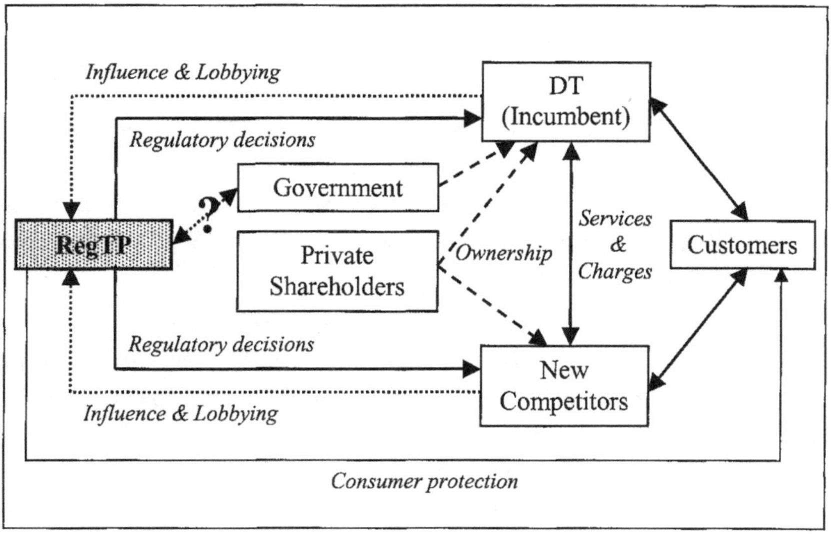

---

[187] *Meibom/ Bussche* (2000) p. 3.
[188] Based on *Geppert/ Ruhle/ Schuster* (1998) p. 572.

The RegTP's task for consumer protection is decreasing in importance to the same extent as consumers gain bargaining power through choice in the market. Important general issues like data protection, secrecy for telecommunications and universal services will remain even after no single firm can execute overwhelming market power.

Both incumbent and competitors are trying to influence regulatory decisions by lobbying. Advantages lie with DT as both RegTP and DT used to be part of the same institution under the former BMPT and personal bonds still exist.

For Government shareholder interests and regulatory power still sometimes collide. For this reason some, mainly foreign, investors have called for a complete sale of all federal shares. RegTP has faced political pressure, especially by the Advisory Council, contradicting its status of independence. Political dependency became obvious as the President's dismissal for party political reasons was discussed after the 1998 change in Government.

Under the TKG the Ministry of Economics and Technology is the body supervising the RegTP. Sec. 66 Para. 5 TKG states that

> "Insofar as the Federal Ministry of Economics gives general directives governing the issue or non-issue of decisions under this Act, such directives shall be published in the Federal Gazette."

This entitles the Ministry to give a ministerial order of general nature to the RegTP. With regards to the telecommunications sector the Ministry has not employed this power so far. This may prove that the Federal Government has respected RegTP's independence. But the Ministry may well employ other measures to defend its interests.

Though the TKG does not provide the Ministry with any further powers of direct intervention in everyday businesses, the Ministry may well influence decisions. For example, in November 1998 the Minister made DT withdraw its application for too high tariffs for unbundled access to its local loop. Hence RegTP had to postpone its ruling on regulated prices, which left competitors longer in a state of insecurity. Though the RegTP should get more self-confidence and respect with every decision, it will have to work hard to reach the status of an independent federal authority as outlined by law. Jurisdiction of the Administrative Courts in lawsuits against the RegTP's decisions will be of crucial importance in this matter.

5.2 Other Regulatory Bodies

Besides the RegTP two other regulatory bodies are working on liberalisation in Germany. Overlapping responsibilities and lack of communication have already caused problems. The major problem of information asymmetry is common to all these cases[189].

5.2.1 The Federal Cartel Office (BKartA)

The Federal Cartel Office (BKartA) generally supervises competition. Under law BKartA and RegTP are required to co-operate in promoting competition. This relationship has not been successful as the BKartA regards regulation by the RegTP partly as interference with its general competence. The BKartA has repeatedly claimed that general matters of competition and liberalisation should be subject to its single general supervision. Conversely the RegTP ignores any competence of the BKartA and avoids involvement as much as possible[190].

This affair is not helped by the fact that appeals against decisions of both authorities have to be made to different courts, which may apply different jurisdiction[191]. For this reason the Monopolies Commission and others argued against a separate and for a unified authority when drafting the TKG[192].

5.2.2 The European Commission

The European Commission watches competition under European competition law, which cannot be restricted by national law. With its decisions and legislation it has, as mentioned above, shaped the national markets. However, the Commission failed to introduce liberalisation in all EU-countries at the same

189 *Stead/ Curwen/ Lawler* (1996) p. 191.
190 *Meibom/ Bussche* (2000) p. 4.
191 *Monopolies Commission* (1996 b) p. 24.
192 *Monopolies Commission* (1996 b) pp. 23 – 25.

pace. Even though there is one single market, some countries have developed much slower[193].

5.3 Regulation at work

When liberalising monopoly regulation is doubtless the precondition to competition. During its first years of work the RegTP has already taken various decisions. Core regulatory issues have been customer prices and the trade with preservices between DT and competitors. Rulings have sometimes been compromises negotiated between DT and its competitors and many of them could only be settled in court.

5.3.1 Regulation on Customer Prices

Since 1997 regulation on customer prices has followed the British price-cap approach[194]. To avoid both limit pricing in competitive and supernormal profits in monopolistic submarkets so far all tariffs offered by DT are subject to the RegTP's prior approval. To determine prices that are eligible for approval, the RegTP uses an analytical cost model in addition to company cost statements and the comparative markets concept. The model takes an element-based approach and establishes the long run incremental costs of the network infrastructure[195]. Based on this some of DT's requests for price reductions, especially for local calls, have been rejected since they were below costs and might hinder entry.

5.3.2 Regulation on Preservices

To offer their services to customers, competitors will have to employ mainly DT preservices until they can rely on their own network structure.

---

[193] See Section 5.5 on Regulation across Europe.

[194] For different methods of regulation of prices and profits see: *Wheatley* (1999) pp. 279 – 287, *Stead/ Curwen/ Lawler* (1996) pp. 190 – 191, *Griffiths/ Wall* (1996) pp. 511 – 518.

[195] *RegTP*, http://www.regtp.de/en/reg_tele/start/fs_05.html, the cost model is outlined under http://www. regtp.de/ en/costmodel/start/fs_12.html

- Interconnection:

  Interconnection of networks is necessary to secure communication between customers of different providers. To make a claim for interconnection operators themselves have to provide the connecting infrastructure. Originally only one such knot was required; to avoid heavy overuse of its network DT now requires one in each of its 23 regional zones in Germany. Investment of providers are encouraged as according to the RegTP, different network operators and providers can be subject to different interconnection rates. If a provider stays below the required number of knots DT can claim additional costs and higher charges than for normal carrier services.

- Carrier Service:

  RegTP decided to lower the price DT (or any other carrier) could charge for carrying competitor's services from 2.7 Pf to an average of 2.04 Pf per minute[196]. Recently RegTP announced the change to an '*element based charging*' model for June 2001 and the prices valid until March 2003[197].

- Access to the local loop:

  Fair and unbundled access to the local loop is vital for competition in the local market. Right from the beginning in accordance with Sec. 2 of the Network Access Ordinance RegTP committed DT to offer access to the local loop to its competitors such that no unsolicited offering needs to be taken (unbundled).

  Finally in February 1999 RegTP fixed the price for the provision of a DT subscriber line for competitors at DM 25.40 per month until March 2001[198]. Competitors, BKartA and the Monopolies Commission criticised this price

---

[196] For detail see press release from 23/12/1999, http://www.regtp.de/aktuelles/start/fs_03.html

[197] For detail see press release from 11/09/2000, http://www.regtp.de/aktuelles/start/fs_03.html, review and discussion of model under http://www.regtp.de/reg_tele/start/fs_05.html

[198] *RegTP* (1999 a) No. 25.

for too high as it is even above the price for standard access paid by customers which is DM 21.39[199].

All regulatory measures put together have sometimes been felt as "overregulation"[200]. The combination of far reaching powers of the RegTP with its lack of experience, its political past and numerous staff, rivalry and lack of co-operation with other regulatory bodies has led to excessive interference.

Despite all activities so far regulation has failed to open the market for local calls to competition. Direct access to customers, however, is vital for sustainable competition and is the most important challenge for regulation in the very near future.

5.4 Chances for Deregulation

In DT's view, regulatory praxis does not sufficiently take the dynamic competitive developments in the sector into account and should begin to phase out regulatory measures[201]. However, in their reports at the end of 1999, both the RegTP[202] and the Monopolies Commission[203] concluded that regulation remains necessary in all areas of the telecommunications market. In its responding statement, published in August 2000, the Federal Government basically agreed, but pointed out that under the TKG price regulation shall phase out without delay as soon as an operator lost its dominant position. Government itself will tighten obligation for network interconnection only to dominant operators[204]. These statements stress the fact that Federal Government is committing itself to competition and deregulation.

After almost three years since complete liberalisation and start of regulation there are already chances for deregulation. As soon as regulation will have successfully created self-sufficient and strong competition, RegTP shall

[199] *Monopolies Commission* (1999) No. 26, prices exclude V.A.T.
[200] *Meiboml Bussche* (2000) p. 4.
[201] *Deutsche Telekom* (2000 a) p. 15.
[202] *RegTP* (1999 b) pp. 190 – 192.
[203] *Monopolies Commission* (1999) No. 70 – 79.
[204] *Federal Government* (2000) pp. 5 – 6.

push towards an increasingly deregulated market. Due to improving sustainability in competition this can be expected very soon for the market of international calls, and for business customers in the middle term. In both markets, DT has lost considerable share to competitors. The RegTP has to enter into deregulation as the next stage despite the fact that this will eventually mean less work for the authority. Here it may be fortunate that RegTP will also be in charge for the liberalisation in the postal market still to come.

However, authorities should act as cautiously with deregulation as with regulation since any measure may well have side effects across the market. Hence, in the middle term sector-specific regulation and legislation seem to be necessary as the EU is following this approach as well. In the long run general competition law shall be applied to telecommunications throughout, finally overcoming the special role this market has played for over a century.

5.5 Regulation across Europe

Table 5.1: Regulatory framework for private companies in some EU-countries[205]

	G	U.K.	F	Italy	Spain	Ireland	Sweden
Open Call-by-Call	Yes	Yes	Yes	Yes	*No*	*No*	Yes
Competition for local calls with unbundled access to local loop	Yes	*No*	*No*	Yes	*No*	*No*	*No*
Number portability	Yes	Yes	Yes	*No*	Yes	*No*	Yes
Approval of tariffs for former monopolist by authority	Yes	Yes	Yes	Yes	Yes	Yes	*No*
Low carrier tariffs	Yes	Yes	Yes	Yes	*No*	Yes	Yes
Low monthly rent for access to local loop	*No*	*No*	Yes	*No*	Yes	*No*	*No*

Regulation and hence telecommunication markets across the EU are far from being a level playing field. Sweden is regarded as the most liberalised

[205] *Wirtschaftswoche* (24/02/2000) p. 124.

country with the U.K. and Germany just behind, while France can be found at the bottom end[206]. Table 5.1 shows that national regulation and legislation have established very different regulatory frameworks.

These differences show that in reality the EU is not a single, but a diverse market. Entry barriers and obligations are very different and liberalisation has been set into force at different paces. For harmonisation the Commission as the European regulatory body should closely, but not as one single authority for the EU, co-ordinate the national bodies. To this end, it should use its legislative and enforcement powers.

Since Europe will loose her advantages over the rest of the world if the pace is not kept up lessons from mobile communications should be learnt. Mobile phones are nowhere else in the world as successful as in Europe for mainly one reason: simple Europe-wide rules and standardisation for GSM were set into force at an early stage, which provided ground for an industry of services and technology to develop. Europe cannot afford to loose her lead in telecommunications as one of the key industries at the beginning of the new millennium.

---

206 Index for liberalisation provided by Mannesmann, *Wirtschaftswoche* (24/02/2000) p. 124.

6 Conclusion

Various institutions and market forces have contributed to the liberalisation process in landlines telecommunications in Germany. During research for this book it became very obvious that these forces have progressed alongside and strongly influenced each other. At the pace of technical progress law and economics together have formed a grid of close links in driving and shaping the market. In the near future present legislation will only be adjusted if necessary for economic or technical reasons.

Germany entered the process of the Postal Reforms very late and at low speed. Only when EU legislation and policy began to push member states towards liberalisation the future of telecommunications became an issue for German authorities. For long they avoided structural changes in the fundamental market constraints, which made several reforms necessary. Due to this lack in political courage much time was wasted for German companies in comparison to their international competitors. But eventually the legislative process gained momentum and the final Telecommunications Act offers complete liberalisation guarded by an open and flexible regulatory framework. The Act has proofed to be an appropriate tool for the difficult transition to competition.

Due to the liberal legal environment the German market has evolved rapidly and is now characterised by fierce competition and diversity in most parts due to low entry barriers and an open market structure. Within the overall growing telecommunications market landlines usage is increasing in volume mainly driven by the Internet. As numbers of main lines reached the point of saturation future growth for landlines can still be expected in volume. Due to mainly price-driven competition revenues have dropped leaving companies with decreasing gain margins. The highest threat to landlines originates from UMTS mobile phones as this technology may advance from complementary to real substitute. But as for other feasible technologies there are a number of uncertainties involved, which may hinder progress in mobiles. The market is developing towards individual converging multimedia solutions. In future these services will be charged in bundles or by data quantity rather than per time.

Deutsche Telekom as the former incumbent is still the giant in German telecommunications, but has lost considerable market share mainly in long-distance, international and mobiles connections to its competitors. Apart from defending its original market against competitors DT's strategy is on the one hand to diversify for new markets and on the other hand to act globally for a broader customer basis. Despite existing constraints from its past DT is well positioned in one of the strongest markets with still potential for growth. Expectations are high for DT remaining one of the world's largest integrated telecommunication companies. For lasting success DT will have to find the right balance in all its ambitions.

Under supervision of the Federal Ministry of Economics and Technology regulation is exercised by the Regulatory Authority, which is vested with far reaching powers by law. So far this body has used its regulatory measures carefully in most cases. Its decisions have mostly been confirmed by the Administrative Courts. This has given the Authority more independence from ministerial supervision. Moreover the Regulatory Authority has tried to make its decision taking process transparent to the public. Twice a year it publishes a general report on progress in the market and all decisions are published in the Federal Gazette. Warnings of the Ministry taking control over regulation by exercising its powers excessively have not come real. Nevertheless in some cases the Ministry has used its influence.

Looking back on the whole process the opening of the telecommunications market in Germany has been an overall success. Once the decision had been made the authorities in charge have supported the process of liberalisation in a very consequent way. This resulted in considerable improvements in market structure in only a short period of time. The changes have been to the benefit of all customers as services of high quality are on offer for far lower prices. Modern technology has been introduced without any delay to the market. Even universal services have so far been provided within the market. Due to rapid fundamental changes Germany has become one of the most liberalised countries for telecommunications. The aim of sustainable and fair competition has been fully achieved in some submarkets.

These positive results have placed trust in the concept of liberalisation. But the difficult task of regulation has also shown the importance of an institution like the Regulatory Authority as a guarantor to liberalisation and deregulation. However, in its work for sector-specific regulation it should concentrate on the unique bottlenecks, which are owed to the fact of former monopoly. For example, to open the local loop to competition will be a crucial task for regulation towards more sustainability of fair competition throughout the market. In this context it has to be criticised that DT has not been forced to sell its cable TV network entirely.

But in a market economy like Germany every sector-specific interference in the market by the state shall not to be continued forever and requires justification for legitimate purposes at any point in time. Therefore, encouraged by this success all involved in the process should work for a phasing-out of sector-specific regulation to move on to the next task: Liberalisation and regulation in the postal market.

Due to restrictions in volume and time this text draws attention to various aspects, but by doing so has to leave consciously others aside. Some of these limitations of this work may provide ideas for future research:

Even though general global perspectives are added to every part of the analysis, it would have been of great interest to compare development in Germany to other countries with greater depth. As pointed out even within the EU national markets have been liberalised and regulated using different approaches. Besides the major players hundreds of small companies are active in the market. Their entrepreneurial chances for niche and general business would have certainly been worth an investigation. The same applies to substitute technologies, where precise analyses of their true cost structure could add valuable results. The Telecommunications Act itself also offers several topics for future research. Issues like the impact of competition in the local loop on the overall market and the regulative measures to achieve it will need substantial academic evaluation as they determine regulatory decisions in practice.

Appendix 1: Chronology of Liberalisation

1971	First attempt towards liberalisation in Germany failed due to heavy resistance of the Postal Union
1982	Change in government to coalition of conservatives and liberals
1885 - 1987	Government Commission on the tasks and possibilities of improving the fulfilment of tasks in telecommunications ('Witte Commission' named after its chairman Eberhard Witte), final report outlines the Postal Reform I
1987	European Commission: 'Towards a Dynamic European Economy, Green Paper on the development of the common market for telecommunications services and equipment', COM(87)290
July 1989	Postal Reform I: **End of monopoly over terminal equipment and most services**
1990	Licences for digital mobile radio networks to DBP Telekom (D1-network) and Mannesmann Mobilfunk GmbH (D2-network) [expanded to the territories of former East Germany in June 1991]
1990 – 1995	Program 'Telekom 2000' for development in former East Germany
28 June 1990	Commission Directive 90/388/EEC on competition in the markets for telecommunications services, and Council Directive 90/387/EEC on the establishment of the internal market for telecommunications services through the implementation of open network provision
3 October 1990	German Reunification Deutsche Post (DP) merge with DBP
May 1993	Third licence for mobile radio network to E-plus Mobilfunk GmbH (E1-network), DCS 1800 standard

22 July 1993	Resolution of the Council of Ministers for Telecommunications on the review of the situation in the telecommunication sector and the need for further development in the market (93/C213/01)
1994	Postal Reform II
	European Commission: 'Towards the Personal Communications Environment: Green Paper on a common approach in the field of mobile and personal Communications in the European Union', COM(94)145
1 January 1995	Start of Deutsche Telekom AG (DT)
August 1996	Telecommunications Act (TKG) in force
	End of monopoly over fixed lines networks
November 1996	Capital increase for DT on international capital markets, first listing and trade of shares on international stock exchanges
1997	Fourth licence for mobile radio network to E2 Mobilfunk GmbH (E2-network, ViagInterkom), DCS 1800 standard
December 1997	European Commission: 'Green Paper on the Convergence of the Telecommunications, Media and Information Technology Sectors, and the Implications for Regulation Towards an Information Society Approach', COM(97)623
31 December 1997	Federal Ministry for Posts and Telecommunications dissolved
1 January 1998	**End of monopoly for voice telephony,**
	Regulatory Authority starts to work: **Begin of Regulation**
5 February 1998	World Trade Organization (WTO) 'General Agreement on Trade in Services (GATS), Fourth Protocol on Basic Telecommunications' entered into force (adopted 30 April 1997) for opening of telecommunication markets
1999	European Commission: 'The 1999 Communications Review: Towards a new Framework for Electronic Communications Infrastructure and associated services', COM(99)539
June 1999	Second capital increase for DT by giving out additional shares

6 March 2000	DT share price reaches highest value so far at € 103.90
April 2000	Floatation of T-Online on the stock exchange
June 2000	First sale of Government shares of DT held by *Kreditanstalt für Wiederaufbau* (*German Development Bank*)
July 2000	DT announced acquisition of VoiceStream, U.S., by 2001
16 August 2000	Federal Government Statement to Regulatory Authority Activity Report and Monopolies Commission Special Report: **Begin of Deregulation of certain submarkets under the TKG**
18 August 2000	T-Mobile secure one of six UMTS licences on German auction
2001?	Floatation of T-Mobile on the stock exchange (Originally scheduled for autumn 2000, but prosponed due to merger)

Appendix 2: The organisational Structure after Postal Reform I[207]

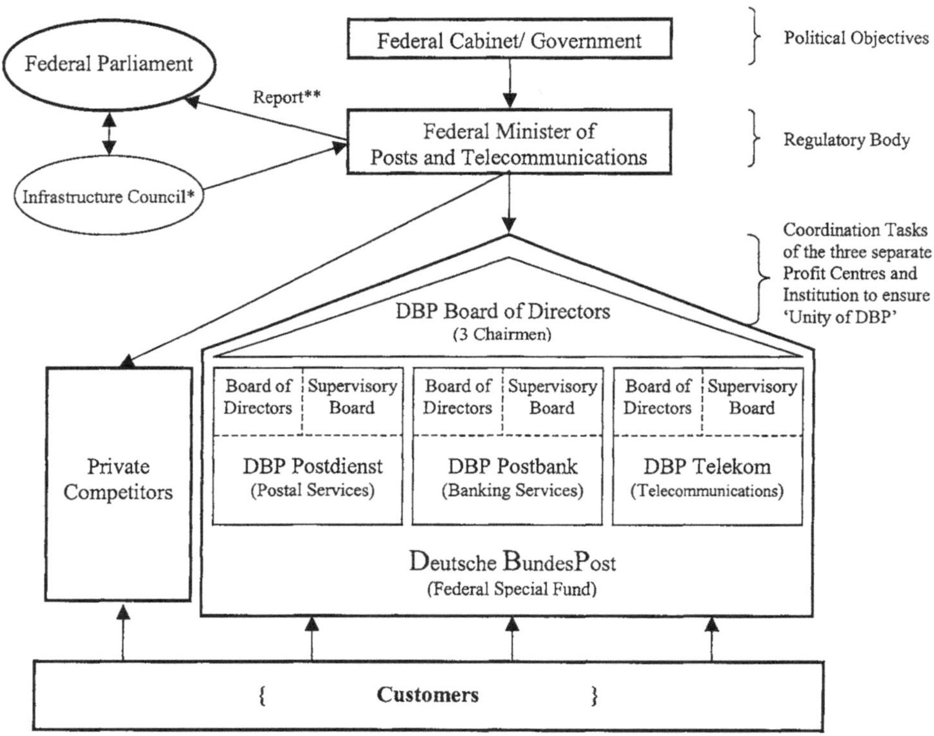

* Infrastructure Council: replaced the former Administrative Council for stimulation of infrastructural obligations, composed of equal number of representatives from Federal Parliament and from Federal Council (originally 11, later 16, making it one for each Federal State).

** Report: submitted to Parliament twice a legislative period.

[207] Based on *Pfeiffer/ Wieland* (1990) p. 14.

Appendix 3: The relevant Articles of the Basic Law (GG)[208] after Postal Reform II

Chapter I Basic Rights

Article 10 [Privacy of letters, posts and telecommunications] – ***unchanged in 1994***

(1) The privacy of letters as well as the secrecy of post and telecommunication is inviolable.

(2) Restrictions may only be ordered pursuant to a statute. Where a restriction serves the protection of the free democratic basic order or the existence or security of the Federation or a State, the statute may stipulate that the person affected shall not be informed and that recourse to the courts shall be replaced by a review of the case by bodies and auxiliary bodies appointed by Parliament.

Chapter VII Federal Legislative Powers

Article 73 [Exclusive legislative power] – ***only wording altered in 1994***

The Federation has exclusive power to legislate in the following matters:

...

7. postal affairs and telecommunication;

...

Chapter VIII Execution of Statutes and Federal Administration

Article 87 [Matters for direct federal administration][209] – ***in force until 1994***

(1) The foreign service, the Federal finance administration, the Federal railroads, the Federal postal service and, in accordance with the provisions of Article 89, the administration of the Federal waterways and of shipping are conducted as matters of Federal administration with their own subordinate administrative structure, ...

---

208 Translation taken from *Würzburg University* at http://www.uni-wuerzburg.de/law/gm00000_.html

209 Translation of this Article taken from http://www.iuscomp.org/gla (*German Law Archive*).

Article 87f [Postal Affairs and Telecommunication] – ***added in 1994***

(1) Regulated by a federal statute requiring the consent of the Senate[210], the Federation guarantees a comprehensive and adequate coverage with services in the area of postal affairs and telecommunication.

(2) Services in the sense of Paragraph (1) are organised as private law activities by those businesses originating in the special property Deutsche Bundespost. Sovereign tasks in the area of postal affairs and telecommunication are organised as direct federal administration.

(3) Notwithstanding Paragraph (2) 2, the Federation, in the public law form of a direct federal agency, discharges certain duties regarding businesses originating in the special property Deutsche Bundespost, as are assigned to it by federal statutes.

Chapter XI Transnational and Concluding Provisions

Article 143b [Businesses of the Former Deutsche Bundespost] – ***added in 1994***

(1) The special property Deutsche Bundespost will be transformed into private law businesses according to a federal statute. The Federation has exclusive legislation over all related matters.

(2) Exclusive rights of the Federation prior to the transformation can be delegated preliminarily to businesses originating in the Deutsche Bundespost POSTDIENST and Deutsche Bundespost TELEKOM. The Federation may sell the majority of shares in the business originating in the Deutsche Bundespost POSTDIENST no earlier than five years after enacting the statute. For this measure, a federal statute with consent of the Senate is required.

(3) Federal officers of the Deutsche Bundespost are being employed by the businesses preserving their legal position and the responsibility of their former employer. These businesses exercise the rights of the former employer. Details are regulated by federal statute.

[210] Note: 'Senate' in this translation used for 'Federal Council'.

Appendix 4: The organisational Structure after Postal Reform II

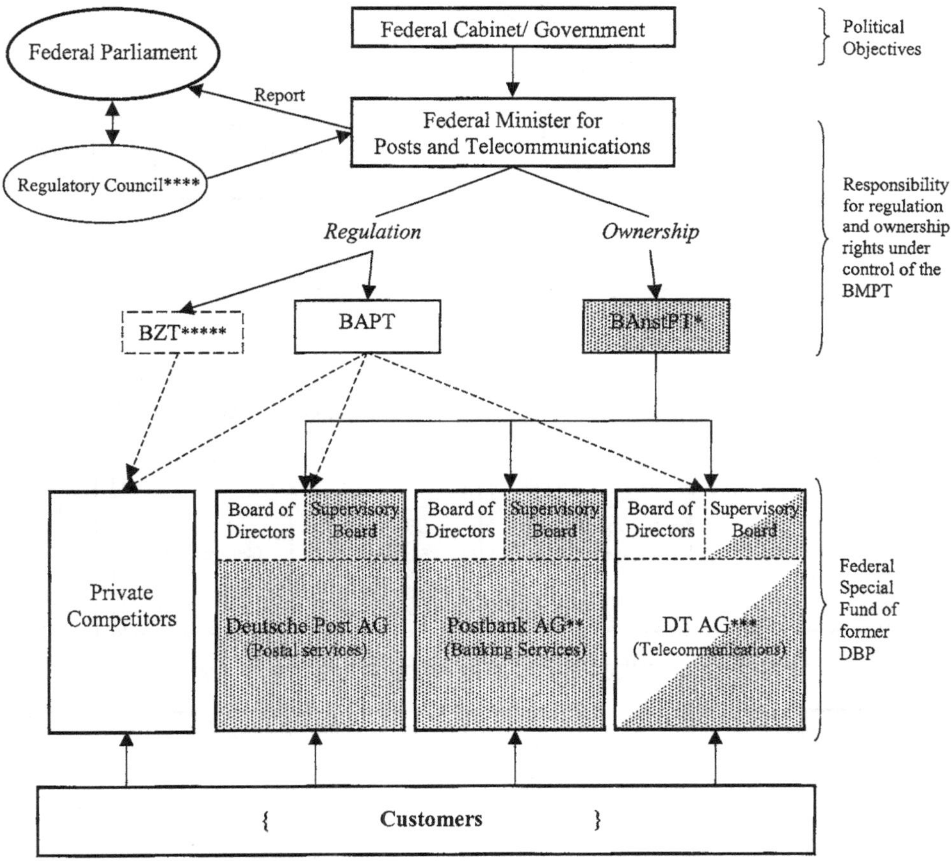

* BAnstPT: Tasks: exercise of shareholder rights, support of IPO, coordination. Board of two Directors and Administrative Council with 10 members: 1 chairperson; 1 representative of each ministry: BMPT, BMWi, and BMF; 1 representative of management and of staff of each company.

** Postbank AG: regulation only under general banking law.

*** Deutsche Telekom AG: partly privatised since November 1996.

**** Regulatory Council: replaced former Infrastructure Council, same composition.

***** BZT: founded as Zentralamt für Zulassungen im Fernmeldewesen (ZZF) in 1982, renamed as BZT in 1992, merged with BAPT in 1996.

Appendix 5: The organisational Structure in 2000

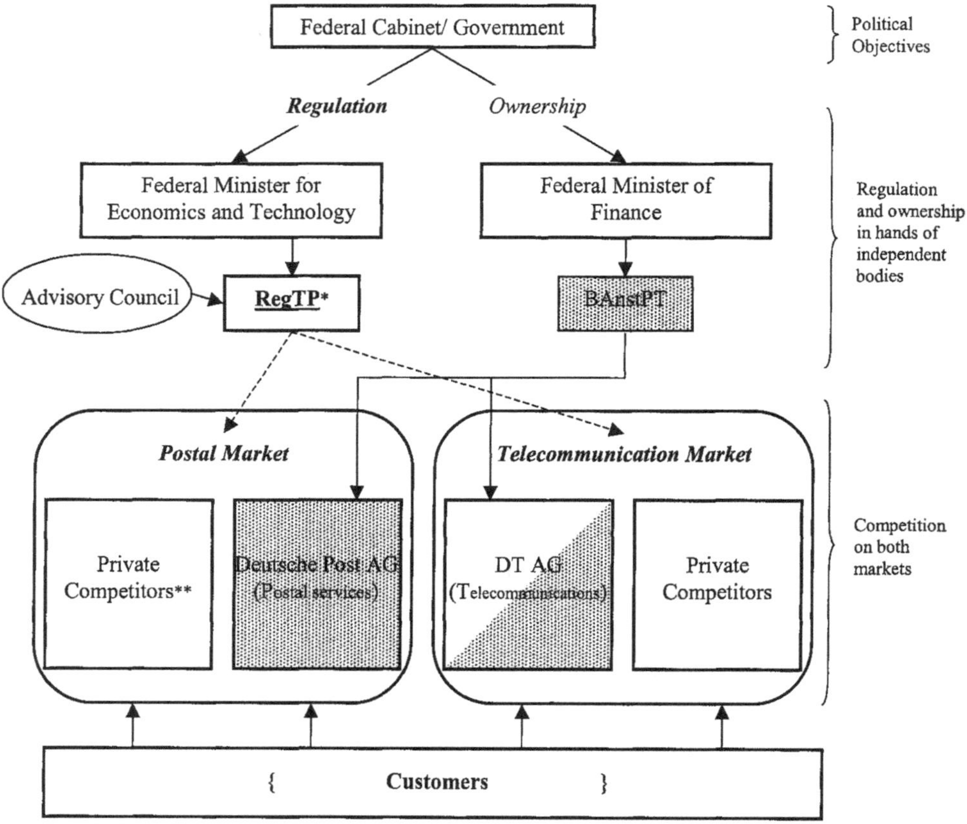

* RegTP: President and vice-presidents appointed by Federal Government;
Decisions made by five Ruling Chambers, cannot be overthrown by the Ministry,
Appeals before the Administrative Courts;
Biannual activity report to Federal Parliament and Federal Council;
48 Regional Offices secure nation-wide presence, headquarters in Bonn.

** Private Competitors: Postal Market has so far only been partly liberalised, monopoly will be sustained until 31 December 2002. Deutsche Post AG still holds 99% market share (*Monopolies Commission* (1999) No. 93).

Appendix 6: Telecommunications in the GDR

Table A6: Differences in Telecommunication Infrastructure in 1989[211]

	East Germany (DP)	West Germany (DBP)
Main Lines	1.8 m	29 m
- Private Main Lines	1.2 m	
- Waiting List	1.2 m 96% for residential lines	0
Main Lines per 100 inhabitants	11	47
Fax Lines	2,500	500,000
Telex Lines	20,000	133,000
Population	16.4 m	62.3 m
GDP per capita (DM)	18,200	38,500

Telecommunication infrastructure was highly underdeveloped under the East German DP: high priority for economic and administrative demand.

Figure A6.1: Ratio of Main Lines and GDP in various countries 1989-1999[212]

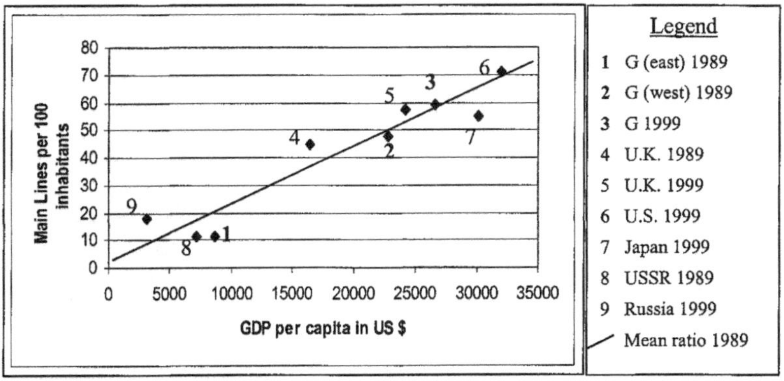

In 1989 the distribution of main lines in East Germany was, even considering low GDP per capita, far below average.

[211] Source: *Schnöring/ Szafran* (1994) p. 9.
[212] Source: *Siemens* (2000) p. 38 and *Schnöring/ Szafran* (1994) p. 8.

Figure A6.2: Switching technology used in East Germany in 1989[213]

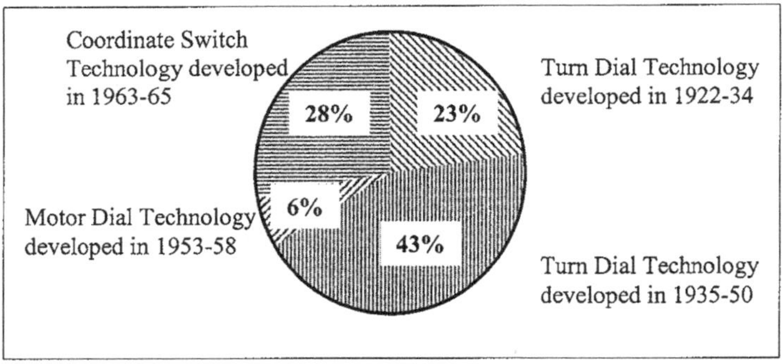

For example, the switching technology employed by DP in the East German network was entirely outdated by 1989.

[213] Source: *Schnöring/ Szafran* (1994) p. 6.

ABBREVIATIONS AND TECHNICAL TERMS

AG	Aktiengesellschaft (*Stock corporation, plc.*)
AktG	Aktiengesetz (*Stock Company Act*)
Art.	Article
ATM	Asynchronous Transfer Mode
Aut	Austria
BAPT	Bundesamt für Post und Telekommunikation (*Federal Department for Posts and Telecommunications*)
BAnstPT	Bundesanstalt für Post und Telekommunikation Deutsche Bundespost (*Federal Institution for Posts and Telecommunications DBP*)
BKartA	Bundeskartellamt (*Federal Cartel Office*)
BMF	Bundesministerium der Finanzen (*Federal Ministry of Finance*)
BMPT	Bundesministerium für Post und Telekommunikation (*Federal Ministry for Posts and Telecommunications, until Dec 31, 1997*)
BMWi	Bundesministerium für Wirtschaft und Technologie (*Federal Ministry for Economics and Technology*)
bn	Billion
BT	British Telecommunications plc.
BZT	Bundesamt für Zulassungen in der Telekommunikation (*Federal Department for Certification in Telecommunications*
Ch	Switzerland
DBP	Deutsche Bundespost (*German Federal Post Office, until Dec 31, 1994*)
DM	Deutsche Mark (DM 1.95583 = € 1 = £ 0.61 *on Sep 1, 2000*)
$	Dollar of the U.S. ($ 0.89 = € 1 *on Sep 1, 2000*)

DP	Deutsche Post (*East German Post Office, merged with DBP on Oct 3, 1990*)
DSL	Digital Subscriber Loop
DT	Deutsche Telekom AG (*after Jan 1, 1995*)
EC	European Community
ECJ	European Court of Justice
e.g.	For example
EU	European Union (*since 1993*)
€	Euro
F	France
FAG	Gesetz über Fernmeldeanlagen, 1927/28 (*Telecommunications Installations Act*)
Federal Council	Bundesrat, representative body of Federal States and second legislative chamber
G	Germany
GDP	Gross Domestic Product
GDR	German Democratic Republic (East-Germany, *until Oct 2, 1990*)
GG	Grundgesetz (*German Basic Law – Federal Constitution*)
GSM	Global System for Mobile communications
GWB	Gesetz gegen Wettbewerbsbeschränkungen (*Act against Restraints to Competition*)
Hun	Hungary
I	Italy
IPO	Initial Public Offering
ISDN	Integrated Services Digital Network
IT	Information Technology
KfW	Kreditanstalt für Wiederaufbau (*German Development Bank*)
km	Kilometre (1.61 km = 1 mile)
LEO	Low Earth Orbit satellite
m	Million

Neue Länder	*Federal States of Mecklenburg-Western Pomerania, Brandenburg, Saxony-Anhalt, Saxony and Thuringia on the ground of the former GDR which joined the Federal Republic of Germany on Oct 3, 1990*
No.	Number
ONP	Open Network Provision
Para.	Paragraph
Pf	Pfennig (DM 1 = 100 Pf)
PLC	Powerline Communications
PSTN	Public Switched Telecommunications Network
RegTP	Regulierungsbehörde für Telekommunikation und Post (*Regulatory Authority for Telecommunications and Posts, since Jan 1, 1998*)
RGSt	Reichsgericht in Strafsachen (*High Court for Criminal Law*)
S	Spain
TelG	Gesetz über das Telegraphenwesen, 1891/92 (*Telegraphy Act*)
TKG	Telekommunikationsgesetz, 1996 (*Telecommunications Act*)
TV	Television
U.K.	United Kingdom of Great Britain and Northern Ireland
UMTS	Universal Mobile Telecommunications System
U.S.	United States of America
USSR	Union of Socialist Soviet Republics (Soviet Union)
Vol.	Volume
WAP	Wireless Application Protocol
WLL	Wireless Local Loop
ZZF	Zentralamt für Zulassungen im Fernmeldewesen (*Central Office of Certification in Telecommunications*)

BIBLIOGRAPHY

Auerbach, Paul (1988) *Competition: The Economics of Industrial Change*. Oxford: Blackwell.

Baggehufwudt, Nils von (1993) "Dienstleistungsmonopole in der Telekommunikation unter EG-rechtlichen Aspekten", in: *Archiv für Post und Telekommunikation*, Vol. 2/ 93, pp. 175 – 179.

Bain, Joe S. (1972) *Essays on Price Theory and Industrial Organization*. Boston: Little, Brown & Com.

Baumol, William J./ Luke W. **Panzar**/ Jared M. **Willig** (1988) *Contestable Markets and the Theory of Industry Structure*, rev. ed. San Diego: Harcourt Brace Jovanovich.

Becker, Lutz (1999) "Entgeltregulierung im TKG unter besonderer Berücksichtigung kartellrechtlicher Preiskontrollinstrumentarien", in: *Kommunikation & Recht*, Vol. 3/ 99, pp. 112 – 123.

Benz, Angelika (1998) "Veränderung staatlicher Aufgabenwahrnehmung durch Privatisierung – das Beispiel Telekommunikation", in: Christoph Gusy (ed.) *Privatisierung von Staatsaufgaben: Kriterien – Grenzen – Folgen*. Baden-Baden: Nomos. Pp. 129 – 164.

Börnsen, Arne (1996) "Das Telekommunikationsgesetz 1996 – Entwicklungen und Hintergründe", in: *Zeitschrift für Gesetzgebung*, 1996, pp. 323 – 343.

Bötsch, Wolfgang (1996) "Zielsetzung und Gestaltungsgrundsätze des neuen Gesetzes", in: Eberhard Witte (ed.) *Das Telekommunikationsgesetz 1996: Eine Herausforderung für Markt und Ordnungspolitik*. Heidelberg: R. v. Decker's Verlag. Pp. 3 – 10.

Bundesverfassungsgericht (BVerfG) in: *Neue Juristische Wochenschrift* (*NJW*), 1978, p. 313.

Burr, Wolfgang (1995) *Netzwettbewerb in der Telekommunikation: Chancen und Risiken aus Sicht der ökonomischen Theorie*. Wiesbaden: Deutscher Universität Verlag.

Darbishire, Owen (1997) "Labor-Mediated Restructuring – Germany", in: Harry C. Katz (ed.) *Telecommunications*. Ithaca: Cornell University Press.

Demsetz, Harold (1968) "Why regulate utilities?", in: *Journal of Law and Economics*, Vol. 11, pp. 55 – 65.

Demsetz, Harold (1982) "Barriers to Entry", in: *The American Economic Review*, Vol. 72, No. 1, pp. 47 – 57.

Deutsche Telekom (1996) *The 1995 Financial Year.* http://www.telekom.de/english/company/inv_rel/gesch_zahlen/index.htm

Deutsche Telekom (1998) *The 1997 Financial Year.* http://www.telekom.de/english/company/inv_rel/gesch_zahlen/index.htm

Deutsche Telekom (2000 a) *The 1999 Financial Year.* http://www.telekom.de/english/company/inv_rel/gesch_zahlen/index.htm

Deutsche Telekom (2000 b) *Half-Year Report of 2000.* http://www.telekom.de/english/company/inv_rel/gesch_zahlen/index.htm

Distelkamp, Martin (2000) *Wettbewerbspotenziale der deutschen Kabel-TV-Infrastruktur*. Bad Honnef: Wissenschaftliches Institut für Kommunikationsdienste.

European Commission (1987) *Towards a Dynamic European Economy: Green Paper on the Development of the Common Market for Telecommunication Services and Equipment*. COM(87)290 final.

European Commission, Eurostat (1997 a) *Panorama of European industry*, Vol. 2, pp. 26-21 – 29.

European Commission (1997 b) *Green Paper on the Convergence of the Telecommunications, Media and Information Technology Sectors, and the Implications for Regulation towards an Information Society Approach.* COM(97)623. http://www.ispo.cec.be/convergencegp/greenp.html

European Commission, Eurostat (1999 a) *Panorama of European enterprises 1999*, Data from 1988 – 99.

European Commission (1999 b) *The 1999 Communications Review: Towards a new Framework for Electronic Communications Infrastructure and associated services.* COM(99)539. http:// www.europa.eu.int/ comm/ information_society/ policy/ telecom/ review99/pdf/review_en.pdf

European Commission (1999 c) *Fifth Report on the Implementation of the Telecommunications Regulatory Package.* http:// www.europa.eu.int/ comm/ information_society/ policy/ telecom/ 5threport/pdf/5threp99ann42_en.pdf

FAZ, Frankfurter Allgemeine Zeitung (*Daily general newspaper*)

Federal Government (2000) *Stellungnahme der Bundesregierung zum Tätigkeitsbericht der Regulierungsbehörde für Post und Telekommunikation 1998/99 und zum Sondergutachten der Monopolkommission „Wettbewerb auf Telekommunikations- und Postmärkten?“*. http://www.bmwi.de

Federal Parliament (1996) "Final debate on the Telecommunications Act", in: *Archiv für Post und Telekommunikation*, Vol. 3/ 96, pp. 275 – 285.

Furse, Mark (1999) *Competition Law of the UK and EC*. London: Blackstone Press

Geppert, Martin/ Ernst-Olav **Ruhle**/ Fabian **Schuster** (1998) *Handbuch Recht und Praxis der Telekommunikation*. Baden-Baden, Nomos.

Griffiths, Alan/ Stuart **Wall** (1996) *Intermediate Microeconomics: Theory and Applications*. Harlow: Longman.

Handelsblatt (*Daily newspaper for economics*)

Herbig, Gottfried (1996) *Die Deutsche Telekom AG: Ein natürliches Monopol auf dem Weg in den europäischen Wettbewerb*, Berichte aus dem Europa-Institut Nr. 333. Saarbrücken: Europa-Institut.

Herres, Jürgen (1994) "Die Post im privatrechtlichen Gewand", in: *Archiv für Post und Telekommunikation*, Vol. 4/ 94, pp. 303 – 311.

Heuermann, Arnulf/ Thomas **Schnöring** (1990) *Vor- und Nachteile einer Trennung von Post- und Fernmeldewesen*. Berlin: Springer.

Hübsch, Hans-Jürgen/ Arndt **Rautenberg** (2000) "Telekommunikation: Der Wettbewerb wird jenseits des Minutenpreises entschieden“, in: *Kommunikation & Recht*, Vol. 2/2000, pp. 79 – 84.

Johnson, Gerry/ Kevan **Scholes** (1997) *Exploring Corporate Strategy, Text and Cases*, 4th ed. London: Prentice Hall.

Königshofen, Thomas (1995) "Die Deutsche Telekom im Spannungsfeld der Ordnungspolitik", in: *Archiv für Post und Telekommunikation*, Vol. 2/ 95, pp. 113 – 127.

Krüger, Reinald/ Gönke **Tetens**/ Axel **Voß** (1995) *Markteintrittsmöglichkeiten und ordnungspolitische Alternativen für deutsche Telekommunikationsmärkte: Gutachten für BMPT*. Baden-Baden: Nomos.

Ladeur, Karl-Heinz (1998) "Regulierung nach dem TKG", in: *Kommunikation & Recht*, Vol. 11/ 98, pp. 479 – 486.

Managermagazin (*Fortnightly magazine for managers*)

Mahrdt, Niklas (1998) *Wettbewerbspolitische Beurteilung strategischer Allianzen beim Angebot digitaler Informations- und Telekommunikationsdienste*. Baden-Baden: Nomos.

Meibom, Wolfgang von/ Axel Freiherr von dem **Bussche** (2000) „How is Liberalisation of Telecommunications Panning Out in Germany?“ in: *European Business Law Review*, Vol. 11, Issue 1, January/ February 2000, pp. 2 – 7.

Merkin, Robert/ Karen Williams (1984) *Competition Law: Antitrust Policy in the U.K. and the EEC*. London: Sweet & Maxwell.

Mobilcom (2000) *Annual Report 1999*. http://www.mobilcom.de/pdf/mc_gb_99.pdf

Monopolies Commission (1991) *Sondergutachten 20: Zur Neuordnung der Telekommunikation (Special Report 20: Restructuring Telecommunications)*. Baden-Baden: Nomos.

Monopolies Commission (1994) *X. Hauptgutachten 1992/93: Mehr Wettbewerb auf allen Märkten*, cited from BTDrucksache 12/8323.

Monopolies Commission (1996 a) *XI. Hauptgutachten 1994/95: Wettbewerbspolitik in Zeiten des Umbruchs*, cited from BTDrucksache 13/5309.

Monopolies Commission (1996 b) *Sondergutachten 24: Telekommunikation im Wettbewerb*. Baden-Baden: Nomos.

Monopolies Commission (1998) *XII. Hauptgutachten 1996/97: Marktöffnung umfassend verwirklichen (12th Biannual Report: Opening up Markets Intensively)*. Baden-Baden: Nomos.

Monopolies Commission (1999) *Sondergutachten 29: Wettbewerb auf den Telekommunikations- und Postmärkten?* http://www.monopolkommission.de/sg_29/text_d.htm

Müller-Terpitz, Ralf (1997) “Die Regulierungsbehörde für den Telekommunikationsmarkt”, in: *Zeitschrift für Gesetzgebung*, 1997, pp. 257 – 274.

Nett, Lorenz (1998) “Price-Cap-Regulierung im Markt für Telekommunikation in Deutschland”, in: *Zeitschrift für öffentliche und gemeinwirtschaftliche Unternehmen*, Vol. 21, pp. 350 – 359.

Ordemann, Klaus-Dieter (1997) “Schaffung der Rahmenbedingungen für einen liberalisierten Telekommunikationsmarkt in Europa ab 1998”, in: *Archiv für Post und Telekommunikation*, Vol. 2/ 97, pp. 109 – 112.

Ossenbühl, Fritz/ Klaus **Ritgen** (1999) *Beamte in privaten Unternehmen: Zum Rechtsstatus der von der Deutschen Telekom AG übernommenen Bundesbeamten*. Baden-Baden: Nomos.

Paulweber, Michael (1999) *Regulierungszuständigkeit in der Telekommunikation*. Baden-Baden: Nomos.

Pfeiffer, Günter/ Bernhard **Wieland** (1990) *Telecommunications in Germany: An Economic Perspective*. Berlin: Springer.

Porter, Michael E. (1980) *Competitive Strategy: Techniques for analyzing industries and competitors*. New York: Free Press.

Regulatory Authority (RegTP) (1999 a) *Jahresbericht 1998*. http://www.regtp.de/aktuelles/start/fs_03.html

Regulatory Authority (RegTP) (1999 b) *Zwei Jahre Telekommunikation- und Postmärkte: Tätigkeitsbericht 1998/ 1999*. http://www.regtp.de/aktuelles/start/fs_03.html

Regulatory Authority (RegTP) (2000 a) *Annual Report 1999*. http://www.regtp.de/en/behoerde/start/fs_01.html

Regulatory Authority (RegTP) (2000 b) *Mid-Year Report 2000*. http://www.regtp.de/en/market/start/fs_15.html

Reichsgericht in Strafsachen, RGSt (Jurisdiction of the German High Court in Criminal Law).

Rottmann, Michael (1994) "Zu den verfassungsrechtlichen Aspekten der Postreform II", in: *Archiv für Post und Telekommunikation*, Vol. 3/ 94, pp. 193 – 197.

Scherer, Joachim/ Torsten **Bartsch** (1998) "Telecommunication Law and Policy of the European Union", in: Joachim Scherer (ed.) *Telecommunication Laws in Europe*, 4th ed. London: Butherworths. Pp. 3 – 55.

Scherer, Joachim/ Ulrich **Ellinghaus** (1998) "Telecommunication Law in Germany", in: Joachim Scherer (ed.) *Telecommunication Laws in Europe*, 4th ed. London: Butherworths. Pp.134 - 154.

Scherer, Joachim (2000) "Entwicklungslinien des Telekommunikationsrechts", in: *Computer und Recht*, Vol. 1/ 2000, pp. 35 – 44.

Scheuerle, Klaus-Dieter/ Gernot **Lehr**/ Thomas **Mayen** (1997) "Einführung", in: *Telekommunikationsrecht, Gesetzestext*. Munich: Beck.

Schmidt, Kurt (1999) "Entgeltregulierung für Telekommunikationsdienstleistungen", in: *Kommunikation & Recht*, Vol. 9/ 99, pp. 385 – 390.

Schmidt, Reiner (1993) "Rechtliche Möglichkeiten für Privatisierungen im Bereich der Deutschen Bundespost", in: Peter Badura/ Rupert Scholz (ed.) *Wege und Verfahren des Verfassungslebens*. Munich: Beck. Pp. 965 – 977.

Schmittmann, Michael (1998) "Wettbewerbsrecht in deregulierten Kommunikationsmärkten", in: *Kommunikation & Recht*, Vol. 1/ 98, pp. 1 – 9.

Schnöring, Thomas/ Uwe **Szafran** (1994) *Entwicklung der Telekommunikation in den neuen Bundesländern: Beispiel einer erfolgreichen Strukturanpassung*. Berlin: Springer.

Schrader, Stephan (1996) „Der neue ordnungspolitische Rahmen für die Telekommunikationsmärkte – Eine Bestandsaufnahme“, in: Eberhard Witte (ed.) *Das Telekommunikationsgesetz 1996: Eine Herausforderung für Markt und Ordnungspolitik*. Heidelberg: R. v. Decker's Verlag. Pp. 35 – 44.

Schwintowski, Hans-Peter (1998) "Ordnung und Wettbewerb auf Telekommunikationsmärkten", in: Ulrich Immenga/ Natalie Lübben/ Hans-Peter Schwintowski (ed.) *Telekommunikation: Vom Monopol zum Wettbewerb*. Baden-Baden: Nomos. Pp.15 – 45.

Siemens AG (2000) *International Telecom Statistics 2000*, status Dec 31, 1999. Munich: Siemens

Sprißler, Matthias (1991) "Das Fernmeldemonopol und seine rechtshistorische Entwicklung in Deutschland", in: *Archiv für Post und Fernmeldewesen*, Vol. 2/ 91, pp. 159 – 177.

Stead, Richard/ Peter **Curwen**/ Kevin **Lawler** (1996) *Industrial Economics: Theory, Applications and Policy*. Maidenhead: McGraw-Hill.

ViagInterkom AG (2000) *Directaccess* (wireless local loop by ViagInterkom). http://www.viaginterkom.de/directaccess/index_direct.html

Weatley, Jeffery J. (1999) *World Telecommunications Economics*, IEE Telecommunications Series 41. London: The Institution of Electrical Engineers.

Wichert-Nick, Dorothea von (1999) *Wettbewerb im lokalen Telekommunikationsmarkt: Zwischen sektorspezifischer Regulierung und Wettbewerbsrecht*. Baden-Baden: Nomos.

Wirtschaftswoche (*Weekly magazine for economics and business*)

List of Tables

LIST OF FIGURES

FSC
www.fsc.org
MIX
Papier | Fördert
gute Waldnutzung
FSC® C083411

Kolibri 360 GmbH
Ferdinand-Jühlke-Straße 7
99095 Erfurt, Deutschland
produktsicherheit@kolibri360.de

Druck:
CPI Druckdienstleistungen GmbH
im Auftrag der
Kolibri 360 GmbH
Ferdinand-Jühlke-Str. 7
99095 Erfurt